John Quincy Adams

Letters on the Masonic Institution

John Quincy Adams

Letters on the Masonic Institution

ISBN/EAN: 9783337816612

Printed in Europe, USA, Canada, Australia, Japan

Cover: Foto ©Thomas Meinert / pixelio.de

More available books at **www.hansebooks.com**

LETTERS AND ADDRESSES

ON

FREEMASONRY.

By JOHN QUINCY ADAMS.

WITH AN INTRODUCTION

BY

CHARLES FRANCIS ADAMS.

"I shall never disavow my old work or shrink from the attribution
of it to my hand, whether in private or in public.
"Very truly yours.   C. F. ADAMS."
3 August. 1875.

DAYTON, OHIO:
UNITED BRETHREN PUBLISHING HOUSE.
1875.

A ³₂

CONTENTS.

APPENDIX.

PREFACE.

This publication of Mr. Adams' Letters on Freemasonry was undertaken because it was believed that so able and valuable a work should again be put in print in a style suitable for a place in libraries. Mr. Adams intensely hated all that he conceived to be wrong, and it will be seen that in these letters he, with all the fervor of his soul, labored to show the wrongs, corruptions, and blasphemies of the lodge. To the decadence of the order these letters greatly contributed; and when, after many years, it began to show signs of reviving Mr. Adams' letters as they appear were published in a neat volume at Boston, with an eloquent introduction by Charles Francis Adams, two pages of which were omitted, as being deemed inappropriate to this publication.

As will be seen by the letter in review of Mr. Sheppard's defense of Freemasonry, Mr Adams endured abuse and misrepresentation long for his Antimasonic views before he came out in public to declare and defend those views.

These letters are mainly a series addressed to Edward Ingersoll, to William L. Stone, and to Edward Livingston. Others not less able, nor scarcely less important, were written to men of national distinction, as William H. Seward, Richard Rush, and Levi Lincoln.

The letters to the committee of the Antimasonic state

convention of Vermont and that of the secretary of the
Antimasonic state convention of Pennsylvania partake
somewhat of the nature of public addresses, to which is
to be added his lengthy and masterly address to the people
of Massachusetts.

It is proper to state that the letters to Colonel William L.
Stone, of New York, were in reply to letters addressed to
him by Mr. Stone in apology, though not in justification, of
the Masonic institution. In these letters he shows most
clearly the absurdity of those apologies by one who, though
he had abandoned the lodge, still had not formally seceded
from the order.

The letters addressed to Hon. Edward Livingston, of
Louisiana, who had accepted the office of general grand
high-priest of the order stands out as a terrible arraignment
of the order, and as a most effective defense of Antimasons
from the imputations made against them.

INTRODUCTION.

The institution of Masonry was introduced into the British colonies of North America more than a hundred years ago. It went on slowly at first; but from the time of the Revolution it spread more rapidly, until in the first quarter of the present century it had succeeded in winding itself through all the departments of the body politic in the United States, and in claiming the sanction of many of the country's most distinguished men. Up to the year 1826 nothing occurred to mar its progress, or to interpose the smallest obstacle to its triumphant success. So great had then become the confidence of the members in its power, as to prompt the loud tone of gratulation in which some of its orators then indulged at their public festivals; and among these none spoke more boldly than Mr. Brainard, in the passage which will be found quoted in the present volume. He announced that Masonry was exercising its influence in the sacred desk, in the legislative hall, and on the bench of justice; but so little had the public attention been directed to the truth he uttered, that the declaration passed off, and was set down by the uninitiated rather as a flower of rhetoric with which young speakers will some-

times magnify their topic, than as entitled to any particularly serious notice. Neither would these memorable
words have been rescued from oblivion, if it had not
happened that the very next year after they were uttered
was destined to furnish a most extraordinary illustration
of their significance.

In a small town situated in the western part of the State
of New York an event occurred in the autumn of the year
1826, which roused the suspicions first of the people living
in the immediate neighborhood, and afterward of a very
wide circle of persons throughout the United States. A
citizen of Batavia suddenly disappeared from his family,
without giving the slightest warning. Rumors were
immediately circulated that he had run away; but there
were circumstances attending the act which favored the
idea that personal violence had been resorted to, although
the precise authors of it could not be distinctly traced.
The name of the citizen who thus vanished as if the earth
had opened and swallowed him from sight, was William
Morgan. He had been a man of little consideration in
the place, in which he had been but a short time resident.
Without wealth,—for he was compelled to labor for the
support of a young wife and two infant children,—and
without influence of any kind, it seemed as if there could
be nothing in the history or the pursuits of the individual
to make him a shining mark of persecution on any
account. So unreasonable, if not absurd, did the notion
of the forcible abduction of such a man appear, that it was
at first met with a cold smile of utter incredulity. Among
the floating population of a newly-settled country, the

single fact of the departure of persons having few ties to bind them to any particular spot would scarcely cause remark or lead to inquiry. Numbers, when first called to express an opinion in the case of Morgan, at once jumped to the conclusion that he had voluntarily fled to parts unknown. So natural was the inference that even to this day many who have never taken any trouble to look into the evidence are impressed with a vague notion that it is the proper solution of the difficulty. In ordinary circumstances the thing might have passed off as a nine days' wonder, and in a month's time the name of Morgan might have been forgotten in Batavia, had it not been for a single clue which was left behind him, and which, at first followed up from curiosity, even excited wonder, and from this led to astonishment at the nature of the discoveries that ensued.

The single clue which ultimately unwound the tangled skein of evidence was this: The sole act of Morgan, while dwelling in Batavia, which formed any exception to the ordinary habits of men in his walk of life, was an undertaking into which he entered, in partnership with another person, to print and publish a book. This book promised to contain a true account of certain ceremonies and secret obligations taken by those who joined the society of Freemasons. The simple announcement of the intention to print this work was known to have been received by many of the persons in the vicinity, acknowledged brethren of the order, with signs of the most lively indignation. And as the thing went on to execution, so many efforts were made to interrupt and to prevent it, even at the hazard of much violence, that soon after the disappearance of the prime mover of the plan doubts began to spread in the community, whether there was not some connection, in the way of cause and effect, between the proposed publication and that event. Circumstances rapidly confirmed suspicion into belief, and belief into certainty. At first the attention was concentrated upon the individuals of the fraternity discovered to have been concerned in the taking off. It afterward spread itself so far as to embrace the action of the lodges of the region in which the deed was done. But such was the amount of resistance experienced to efforts made to ferret out the perpetrators and bring them to justice, that ultimately the whole organization of the order became involved in responsibility for the misdeeds of its members. The opposition made to investigation only stimulated the passion to investigate. Unexampled efforts were made to enlist the whole power of the social system in the pursuit of the kidnappers, which were as steadily baffled by the superior activity of the Masonic power. In time it became plain that the only effectual course would be to go, if possible, to the root of the evil, and to attack Masonry in its very citadel of secret obligations.

The labor expended in the endeavor to suppress the publication of Morgan's book proved to have been lost. It came out just at the moment when the disappearance of its author was most calculated to rouse the public curiosity to its contents. On examination, it was found to contain what purported to be the forms of oaths taken by those who were admitted to the first three degrees of

Masonry—the Entered Apprentice's, the Fellowcraft's, and the Master Mason's. If they really were what they pretended to be, then indeed was supplied a full explanation of the motives that might have led to Morgan's disappearance. But here was the first difficulty. Doubts were sedulously spread of their genuineness. Morgan's want of social character was used with effect to bring the whole volume into discredit. Neither is it perfectly certain that its revelations would have been ultimately established as true, had not a considerable number of the fraternity, stimulated by the consciousness of the error which they had committed, voluntarily assembled at Leroy,—a town in the neighborhood of Batavia,—and then and there, besides attesting the veracity of Morgan's book, renounced all further connection with the society. One or two of these persons subsequently made far more extended publications, in which they opened all the mysteries of the Royal Arch, and of the Knight Templar's libation, besides exposing in a clear light the whole complicated organization of the institution. Upon these disclosures the popular excitement spread over a large part of the northern section of the Union. It crept into the political divisions of the time. A party sprung up almost with the celerity of magic, the end of whose exertions was to be the overthrow of Masonry. It soon carried before it all the power of western New York. It spread into the neighboring states. It made its appearance in legislative assemblies, and there demanded full and earnest investigations, not merely of the circumstances attending the event which originated the excitement, but also of the nature of the

obligations which Masons had been in the habit of
assuming. Great as was the effort to resist this movement,
and manifold the devices to escape the searching operation proposed, it was found impossible directly to stem
the tide of popular opinion. Masons who stubbornly
adhered to the order were yet compelled under oath to
give their reluctant testimony to the truth of the disclosures
that had been made. The oaths of Masonry, and the
strange rites practiced simultaneously with the assumption
of them, were then found to be in substance what they
had been affirmed to be. The veil that hid the mystery
was rent in twain, and there stood the idol before the gaze
of the multitude, in all the nakedness of its natural
deformity.

Strange though it may seem, it is nevertheless equally
certain, that the most revolting features of the obligations,
the pledges subversive of all moral distinctions, and the
penalties for violating those pledges, were not those things
which roused the most general popular disapprobation.
Here, as often before, the shield of private character,
earned by a life and conversation without reproach, was
interposed with effect to screen from censure men who
protested that when they swore to keep secret the crimes
which their brethren might have committed, provided
they were revealed to them under the Masonic sign, they
did nothing which they deemed inconsistent with their
duties as Christians and as members of society. It is the
tendency of mankind to mix with all abstract reasoning,
however pure and perfect, a great deal of the alloy of
human authority, to harden its nature. Multitudes pre-

ferred to believe the Masonic oaths and penalties to be ceremonies, childish, ridiculous, and unmeaning, rather than to suppose them intrinsically and incurably vicious. They refused to credit the fact that men whom they respected as citizens could have made themselves parties to any promise whatsoever to do acts illegal, unjust, and wicked. Rather than go so far, they preferred to throw themselves into a state of resolute unbelief of all that could be said against them. Hence the extraordinary resistance to all projects of examination, that great wall of brass which the conservative temper of society erects around acknowledged and time-hallowed abuses. Hence the determination to credit the assurances of interested witnesses, who seemed to have a character for veracity to support, rather than by pressing investigation, to undermine the established edifice constructed by the world's opinion.

Neither is there at bottom any want of good sense, in this sluggish mode of viewing all movements of reform. Agitation always portends more or less of risk to society, and tends to bring mere authority into contempt. It is therefore not without reason that those who value the security which they enjoy under existing institutions hes - tate at adopting any rule of conduct which may materially diminish it. Such hesitation is visible under all forms of government; but it is nowhere more marked than in the United States, where the popular nature of the institutions makes the tendency to change at all times imminent. The misfortune attending this natural and pardonable con- servative instinct is, that it clings with indiscriminate

tenacity to all that has been long established—the evil as
well as the good, the abuses that have crept in equally
with the useful and the true. It was just so in the case of
Masonry. A large number of the most active and respected members of society had allowed themselves to
become involved in its obligations, and rather than
voluntarily to confess the error they had committed, and
to sanction the overthrow of the institution by a decided
act of surrender, they preferred to support it upon the
strength of their present character, and upon the
combination of themselves and the friends whom they
could influence to resist the assaults of a reforming and
purifying power. Great as was the strength of this resistance, it could only partially succeed in accomplishing
the object at which it aimed. The opposition made to
the admission of a palpable moral truth had its usual and
natural effect to stimulate the efforts of those who were
pressing it upon the public attention. Admitting in the
fullest extent everything that could be said in behalf of
many of the individuals who as Masons became subjected
to the vehemence of the denunciations directed against the
fraternity, it was yet a fact not a little startling that even
they should deem themselves so far bound by unlawful
obligations as at no time to be ready to signify the
smallest disapprobation of their character, not even after
the fact was proved how much of evil they had caused.
After the disclosure of the Morgan history it was no
longer possible to pretend that the pledges were not
actually construed in the sense which the language plainly
conveyed. That after admitting the possibility of such a

construction the association which for one moment longer should give it countenance made itself responsible for all the crime which might become the fruit of it, can not be denied. Yet this reasoning did not appear to have the weight to which it was fairly entitled, in deterring the respectable members of the society from giving it their aid and countenance. De Witt Clinton still remained Grand Master of the order after he had reason to know the extent to which it had made itself accessory to the Morgan murder. Edward Livingston was not ashamed publicly to declare his acceptance of the same office, although the chain of evidence which traced that crime to the Masonic oath had then been made completely visible to all. When the authority of such names as these was invoked with success to shelter the association from the effect of its own system, it seemed to become an imperative duty on the part of those whose attention had been aroused to the subject to look beyond the barrier of authority so sedulously erected in order to keep them out, to probe by a searching analytic process the moral elements upon which the institution claimed to rest, and to concentrate the rays of truth and right reason upon those corrupt principles which, if not effectively counteracted, seemed to threaten the very foundations of justice in the social and moral system of America.

It was the province here marked out which Mr. Adams voluntarily assumed to fill when he addressed to Colonel William L. Stone that series of letters upon the Entered Apprentice's oath, which will be found to make a part of the present volume. Although this obligation may be

considered as constituting the lowest story and least
commanding portion of the edifice of Freemasonry, yet he
singled it out for examination as the fairest test by which
he could try the merits of all that has been built above it.
If that first and simple step proved untenable, it followed,
as a matter of course, that no later or more difficult one
could fare a whit better. Of the result of the investigation thus entered into, it is thought that no difference of
opinion can now be entertained. No answer worthy of a
moment's consideration was ever made. It is confidently
believed that none is possible. As a specimen of rigid
moral analysis the letters must ever remain —not simply
as evincing the peculiar powers of the author's mind, but
also as a standing testimony against the radical vice of
the secret institution against which they were directed.

When the books of Morgan, and Allyn, and Bernard,
the admissions of Colonel Stone and of the Rhode Island
legislative investigation, had left little of the mysteries of
Freemasonry unseen by the public eye, the impressions
derived from observation were curious and contradictory.
Upon the first hasty and superficial glance a feeling might
arise of surprise that the frivolity of its unmeaning ceremonial, and the ridiculous substitution of its fictions for
the sacred history, should not have long ago discredited
the thing in the minds of good and sensible men everywhere. Yet upon a closer and more attentive examination this first feeling vanishes, and makes way for astonishment at the ingenious contrivance displayed in the
construction of the whole machine. A more perfect
agent for the devising and execution of conspiracies

against church or state could scarcely have been conceived. At the outer door stands the image of secrecy,
stimulating the passion of curiosity. And the world which
habitually takes the unknown to be sublime, could scarcely
avoid inferring that the untold mysteries which were supposed to have been transmitted undivulged to any external
ear, from generation to generation, must have in them
some secret of power richly worth the knowing. Here
was the temptation to enter the portal. But the unlucky
wight, like him of the poet's hell, when once admitted
within the door, was doomed at the same moment to leave
behind him all hope or expectation of retreat. His mouth
was immediately sealed by an obligation of secrecy, imposed with all the solemnity that can be borrowed from
the use of the forms of religious worship. Nothing was
left undone to magnify the effect of the scene upon his
imagination. High-sounding titles, strange and startling
modes of procedure, terrific pledges and imprecations,
and last, though not least, the graduation of orders in an
ascending scale, which, like mirrors placed in long vistas,
had the effect of expanding the apparent range of vision
almost to infinitude, were all combined to rescue from
ridicule and contempt the moment of discovery of the
insignificant secret actually disclosed. Having thus been
tempted by curiosity to advance, and being cut off by
fear from retreat, there came last of all the appearance
of a sufficient infusion of religious and moral and benevolent profession to furnish an ostensible cause for the
construction of a system so ponderous and complicate.
The language of the Old Testament, the history as well as

the traditions of the Jews, and the resources of imagination, are indiscriminately drawn upon to deck out a progressive series of initiating ceremonies which would otherwise claim no attribute to save them from contempt. Ashamed and afraid to go backward, the novice suffers his love of the marvelous, his dread of personal hazard, and his hope for more of the beautiful and the true than has yet been doled out to him, to lead him on until he finds himself crawling under the living arch, or committing the folly of the fifth libation. He then too late discovers himself to have been fitting for the condition either of a dupe or of a conspirator. He has plunged himself needlessly into an abyss of obligations, which, if they signify little, prove him to have been a fool, and if, on the contrary, they signify much, prove him ready, at a moment's warning, to make himself a villain.

Such is the impression of the Masonic institution that must be gathered from all the expositions that have been lately made. Yet, strange though it may seem, there is no reason to doubt that the society has had great success in enrolling numbers of persons in many countries among its members, and keeping them generally faithful to the obligations which it imposed. This, if no other fact, would be sufficient to relieve the whole machine from the burden of ridicule it might otherwise be made to bear. Perhaps the strongest feature of the association is to be found in the pledge it imposes of mutual assistance in distress. On this account much merit has been claimed to it, and many stories have been circulated of the benefits which individuals have experienced in war, or in perils by sea and land, or in other disasters, by the ability to resort to the grand hailing sign. This argument, which has probably made more Freemasons than any other, would be good in its defense were it not for two objections. One of them is, that the pledge to assist is indiscriminate, making little or no difference between the good or bad nature of the actions to promote which a co-operation may be invoked. The other is, that the engagement implies a duty of preference of one member of society to the disadvantage of another who may be in all respects his superior. It establishes a standard of merit conflicting with that established by the Christian or the social system, either or both of which ought to be of paramount obligation. And this injurious preference is the more dangerous because it may be carried on without the knowledge of the sufferers. The more scrupulously conscientious a citizen may be, who hesitates at taking an oath the nature of which he does not know beforehand, the more likely will he be to be kept down by the artificial advancement of others who may derive their advantage from a cunning use of their more flexible sense of right. That these are not altogether imaginary objections, there is no small amount of actual evidence to prove. There has been a time when resort to Masonry was regarded as eminently favorable to early success in life; and there have been men whose rapidity of personal and political advancement it would be difficult to explain by any other cause than this, that they have been generally understood to be bright Masons. Such a preference as is here supposed can be justifiable only upon the supposition that

Masonic merit and social merit rest on the same general
foundation—a supposition which no person will be able
to entertain for a moment after he shall have observed
the scales which belong respectively to each.

Another argument which has been effectively resorted to
as an aid to Freemasonry is drawn from its supposed
antiquity.   To give color to this notion, a very ingenious
use has been made of much of the sacred history ; but it
appears to have no solid foundation whatsoever.   Whatever may have been the nature of the associations of
Masons who built the gothic edifices of the middle ages,
the investigations entered into by those who opposed
speculative Freemasonry sufficiently proved that the latter
scarcely dates beyond the early part of the last century.
The air of traditionary mystery, like the *ærugo* on many a
pretended coin, has been artificially added to heighten
its value to the curious.   Yet such has been its effect, that
this cause alone has probably contributed very largely to
fill up the ranks of the society.   The rapidity of its growth
during the period of its legitimate existence is one of the
most surprising circumstances attending its history.   Origi-
nating in Great Britain somewhere about the beginning
of the eighteenth century (1717) it soon ramified not only
in that country, but into France and Germany ; it spread
itself into the colonies of North America, and made its
way to the confines of distant Asia. Although the seeds
of the institution were early planted in Boston and
Charleston, they did not fructify largely until after the
period of the Revolution. The original form of Masonry
was comprised in what are now called the first three

degrees,—the Entered Apprentice, Fellowcraft, and Master,—but during the first quarter of the present century, so thoroughly had the basis been laid over the entire surface of the United States, that the degrees have been multiplied more than tenfold, and in all directions the materials have been collected for a secret combination of the most formidable character. It was not until the history of Morgan laid open the consequences of the abuse of the system, that the public began to form a conception of the dangerous fanaticism which it was cherishing in its bosom. Even then, the endeavor to apply effective remedies to the evil was met with the most energetic and concerted resistance, and the result of the struggle was by no means a decided victory to the opponents of the institution.* Freemasonry still lives and moves and has a being, even in New York and Massachusetts. And at the seat of the federal government, Freemasonry at this moment claims and obtains the privilege of laying the corner-stone of the national institution created upon the endowment of James Smithson, for the purpose of increasing and diffusing knowledge among men.

An obvious danger attending all associations of men connected by secret obligations, springs from their susceptibility to abuse in being converted into engines for the overthrow or the control of established governments. So soon was the apprehension of this excited in Europe by Freemasonry, that many of the absolute monarchies took early measures to guard against its spread within their limits. Rome, Naples, Portugal, Spain, and Russia

*This was written over twenty-five years ago.

made participation in it a capital offense. Other governments more cautiously confined themselves to efforts to
control it by a rigid system of supervision. In Great
Britain the endeavor of government has been to neutralize
its power to harm, by entering into it and by placing
trustworthy members of the royal family at its head. Yet
even with all these precautions and prohibitions, it is
believed that in France at the period of the Revolution,
and in Italy within the present century, much of the
insurrectionary spirit of the time was fostered, if not in
Masonic lodges, at least in associations bearing a close
affinity to them in all essential particulars. With regard
to the United States, there has thus far in their history
been very little to justify any of the most serious objections
which may be made against Masonry in connection with
political affairs. Yet the events which followed the death
of Morgan first opened the public mind to the idea that
already a secret influence pervaded all parts of the body
politic, with which it was not very safe for an individual
to come into conflict. The boast of Brainard, already
alluded to, was now brought to mind. It was found to
bias, if not to control, the action of officers of justice of
every grade, to affect the policy of legislative bodies, and
even to paralyze the energy of the executive head. This
power, by gaining a greater appearance of magnitude
from the mystery with which it was surrounded, was
doubtless much exaggerated by the popular fancy during
the period of the Morgan excitement; but after making
all proper allowances, it is impossible from a fair survey
of the evidence to doubt that it was something real, and

that it might, in course of time, have established an undisputed control over the affairs of the Union, had not its progress been somewhat roughly broken by the consequences of the violent movement against Morgan, which had its origin in the precipitate but fanatical energy of one division of the society. And even since the agitation of that day, there is the best reason for believing that throughout the region most affected by it an organization was made up after the fashion of Masonic lodges, the object of which was directly to stimulate a concerted insurrection against the governing power of a neighboring country, Canada, calculated to give rise to a furious contest with a foreign nation, and to mature plans by which such an attempt could be most effectually aided by citizens of the United States in spite of all the national declarations of neutrality and in defiance of all the fulminations of government at home.

But at the time of Morgan's mysterious disappearance, the investigations then pursued, imperfect as they were, and more than once completely baffled for the moment, brought forth the names of sixty-nine different individuals, many of them of great respectability of private character, who had been directly concerned in the outrages attending his taking off. These sixty-nine persons were not living within a confined circle. They had their homes scattered along an extent of country of at least one hundred miles. That so many men, at so many separate points, should have acted in perfect concert in such a business as they were engaged in, would scarcely be believed without compelling the inference of some distinct understanding exist-

ing between them. That they should have carried into
effect the most difficult part of their undertaking, a scheme
of the most daring and criminal nature, in the midst of a
large, intelligent, and active population, without thereby
incurring the risk of a full conviction of their guilt and the
consequent punishment, would be equally incredible but
for the light furnished by the phraseology of the Masonic
oath. The several forms of this oath, as shown to have
been habitually administered in the first three degrees, will
be found in the appendix to the present volume. These,
together with the ceremony attending the Royal Arch
and the Knight Templar's obligation, have been deemed
all of Masonry that is necessary to illustrate the letters of
Mr. Adams. They are believed sufficient to account for
the successful manner in which Morgan was spirited away.
It is not deemed expedient to dwell here upon their
nature, when it will be found fully analyzed in the body
of the present volume. It is enough to point out the fact
that obedience to the order is the paramount law of association ; that it makes every social, civil, and moral duty
a matter of secondary consideration ; that it draws few
distinctions between the character of the acts that may be
required to be done, and that it demands fidelity to guilt
just the same as if it were the purest innocence. Every
man who takes a Masonic oath forbids himself from
divulging any criminal act, unless it might be murder or
treason, that may be communicated to him under the
seal of the fraternal bond, even though such concealment
were to prove a burden upon his conscience and a violation
of his bounden duty to society and to his God. The

best man in the world, put in this situation, may be compelled to take his election between perjury on one side and sympathy with crime on the other. The worst man in the world, put in this situation, has it in his power to claim that the best shall degrade his moral sense down to the level of his own, by hearing from him, without resentment, revelations to which even listening may be a participation of dishonor.

The facts attending the abduction of Morgan, not elicited without the most extraordinary difficulty by subsequent investigation, have been so often published far and wide as to make it superfluous here to repeat them. It may be enough to state that from the day when the partnership between Morgan and David C. Miller, a printer of Batavia, made for the purpose of publishing the "Illustrations of Masonry," was announced, no form of annoyance which could be expected to deter them from prosecuting their design was left unattempted. The precise nature of these forms may be better understood if we class them under general heads, until they took the ultimate shape of aggravated crime.

1. Anoymous denunciation of the man Morgan, as an impostor, in newspapers published at Canandaigua, Batavia, and Black Rock, places at some distance from each other, but all within the limits of the region in which the subsequent acts of violence were committed.

2. Abuse of the forms of law, by the hunting up of small debts or civil offenses with which to carry on vexatious suits or prosecutions against the two persons heretofore named.

3. The introduction of a spy into their counsels, and of a traitor to their confidence, employed for the purpose of betraying the manuscripts of the proposed work to the Masonic lodges, and thus of frustrating the entire scheme.

4. Attempts to surprise the printing-office by a concerted night attack of men gathered from various points, assembling at a specific rendezvous, the abode of a high member of the order, and proceeding in order to the execution the object, which was the forcible seizure of the manuscripts and the destruction of the press used to print them.

5. Efforts to get possession of the persons of the two offenders, by a resort to the processes of law, through the connivance and co-operation of officers of justice, themselves Masons. These efforts failed in the case of Miller, but they succeeded against Morgan, and were the means by which all the subsequent movements were carried into execution.

6. The employment of an agent secretly to prepare materials for the combustion of the building which contained the printing materials known to be employed in the publication of the book and to set them on fire.

Such were the proceedings which were resorted to at the very onset of this conspiracy; and upon looking at them it will be seen at a glance that the prosecution of them involved the commission of a variety of moral and social offenses, the commission of which *may be fairly included within the literal injunction of the Masonic oath.* Had the matter stopped here it would have furnished abundance of evidence to establish the dangerous character of a secret institution, when its interests are deemed to conflict with those of individual citizens or of society at large. But what has thus far been compressed in the six preceding heads appears as nothing when compared with the startling developments of the remainder of the story.

On Sunday,—of all the days in the week,—the tenth of September, 1826, the coroner of the county of Ontario, himself master of the lodge at Canandaigua, applied to a Masonic justice of the peace of that town for a warrant to apprehend William Morgan, living fifty miles off at Batavia. The offense upon which the application was based was larceny, and the alleged' larceny consisted in the neglect of Morgan to return a shirt and cravat that had been borrowed by him in the previous month of May. Armed with this implement of justice—which assumes in this connection the semblance of a dagger rather than of its ordinary attribute a sword—the coroner immediately proceeded in a carriage, obtained at the public cost, to pick up at different stations along the road of fifty miles ten Masonic brethren, including a constable, anxious and willing to share in avenging the insulted majesty of the law. At the tavern of James Ganson, six miles from Batavia, the same place which had been the head-quarters of the night expedition against Miller's printing-office, the party stopped for the night. Had that expedition proved successful, it is very probable that this one would have been abandoned. As it was, the failure acted as a stimulus to its further prose-cution. Early next morning five of the Masonic beagles, headed by the Masonic constable, having previously procured a necessary indorsement of their writ, to give it effect in the county of Genesee, from a Masonic justice of the peace, proceeded from Ganson's house to Batavia, where they succeeded in seizing and securing the man guilty of the allged enormity touching the borrowed shirt and cravat. A coach was again employed, the Masonic party lost no time in securing their prey, and at about sunset of the same day with the arrest, that is, Monday, the eleventh day of September, they got back to Canandaigua. The prisoner was immediately taken before the justice who had issued the warrant, the futility of the complaint was established, and Morgan was forthwith discharged. The case affords a striking illustration of the abuse of the remedial process of the law to the more secure commission of an offense against law. Morgan was free, it is true, but he was at a distance of fifty miles from home, alone, and without friends, brought through the country with the stigma resulting from the suspicion of a criminal offense attached to him, and all without expense to the parties engaged in the undertaking, as well as without the smallest hazard of a rescue.

.It turned out that the person of whom the shirt and cravat had been originally borrowed had never sought to instigate a prosecution for the offense. The idea originated in the mind of the Masonic coroner himself. He had executed the plan of using the law to punish an offense of Masonry, to the extent to which it had now been carried. Morgan had been brought within the coil of the serpent, but he was not yet entirely at its mercy. Another abuse of legal forms yet remained to complete the operation. No sooner was the victim landed upon the pavement, exonerated from the charge of being a thief, than he found the same Masonic grand master and coroner tapping him on the shoulder, armed with a writ for a debt of two dollars to a tavern-keeper of Canandaigua. Resistance was useless. Morgan had neither money nor credit, and for the want of them he was taken to the county jail. The common property and the remedial process of the state was thus once more employed to subserve the vindictive purposes of a secret society.

Twenty-four hours were suffered to pass, while the necessary arrangements were maturing to complete the terrible drama. On the evening of the succeeding day, being the twelfth of September, the same grand master coroner once more made his appearance at the prison. After some little negotiation Morgan is once more released, by the payment of the debt for which he had been taken. But he is not free. No sooner is he treading the soil of freedom, and perchance dreaming of escaping from all these annoyances, than upon a given signal a yellow carriage and grey horses are seen by the bright moonlight rolling with extraordinary rapidity toward the jail. A few minutes pass; Morgan has been seized and gagged and bound and thrown into the carriage, which is now seen well filled with men, rolling as rapidly as before, but in a contrary direction. Morgan is now completely in the power of his enemies. The veil of law is now removed. All that remains to be done is to use the arm of flesh. Morgan is now taking his last look of the town of Canandaigua.

It is a fact that this carriage moved along, night and day, over a hundred miles of well-settled country, with fresh horses to draw it supplied at six different places, and with corresponding changes of men to carry on the enterprise, and not the smallest let or impediment was experienced. With but a single exception, every individual concerned in it was a Freemason, bound by the secret tie; and the exception was immediately initiated by a unanimous vote of the lodge at Lewiston. It afterward appeared in evidence that the lodge at Buffalo had been called to deliberate upon it, and moreover that the lodges at Le Roy, Bethany, Covington, and Lockport, as well as the chapter at Rochester, had all of them consulted upon it. There is no other way to account for the preparation made along the line of the road traveled by the party. Nowhere was there delay, or hesitation, or explanation, or discussion. Everything went on like clock-work, up to the hour of the evening of the fourteenth of September, when the prisoner was taken from the carriage at Fort Niagara, an unoccupied military post near the mouth of the river of that name, and lodged in the place originally designed for a powder magazine, when the position had been occupied by the troops of the United States. The jurisdiction was now changed from that of the state to that of the federal government, but the power that held the man was one and the same. It was Masonry that opened the gates of the fort, by controlling the will of the brother who for the time had it intrusted to his charge.

On this same evening there was appointed to take place at the neighboring town of Lewiston an installation of a chapter misnamed benevolent, at which the arch-conspirator was to be made grand high-priest, and an opportunity was given to all associates from distant points to come together, and to consult upon what it was best to do next. Here it is, that in spite of the untiring labors of an investigating committee organized for the purpose, and in spite of the entire application of the force of the courts of the country to the eliciting of the truth, and details of the affair which thus far have been clearly exposed, begin to grow dim and shadowy. There is reason to believe that Morgan was carried across the river in a boat at night, and placed at the disposal of a Canadian lodge at Newark. The scruples of one or two brethren, who hesitated at the idea of murder, brought on a refusal to assume the trust. Consultations on this side of the river followed, and messengers were dispatched to Rochester for advice. The final determination was that Morgan must die, to pay the penalty of his violated oath. After this, everything attending the catastrophe becomes more and more uncertain. It is affirmed that eight Masons met and threw into a hat as many lots, three of which only were marked. Each man then drew a lot, and where it was not a marked lot, he went immediately home.* There is reason to believe that the three who remained were the persons who on the night of the 19th or 20th of September took their victim from the fort, where he had been kept for sacrifice, carried him in a boat to the middle of the stream, and,

---

*This is now fully confirmed by the testimony on his death-bed of H. Vallance, of Racine, Wisconsin, one of the three actual murderers of Morgan.

having fastened upon him a heavy weight, precipitated him into eternity.

Such is a condensed statement of this eventful history —a history which in many of its details will vie in interest with any narrative of romance. That such a tragedy *could* be executed in the United States, a country fortified, as the people fondly imagine, by all known securities to life and liberty; that it could be carried on through a period of ten days, in a populous Christian community, without thought of rescue; that it could enlist as actors so large a number of citizens of good repute, in so many different quarters, as were members of the various lodges privy to the transaction; and finally, that it could secure the co-operation of the chosen ministers of justice, and even of some set apart to the service of the Deity, one of whom could be found bold enough to invoke the blessing of God upon the contemplated violation of his most solemn law; that it could involve all these possibilities, was a thing well calculated to rouse the human mind to a high pitch of wonder, until the problem found its natural solution in the disclosure of the Masonic oath. Construed as this obligation was construed by the members of the order in western New York, all cause of surprise at the consequences instantly disappears.

Yet, strange as is this narrative, fearful as is the disclosure of the fanaticism of secret association which could impel men holding a respectable rank in society, walking by the light of modern civilization, acknowledging the influence of Christianity over their daily life, to the commission of outrages so flagrant as were the abduction and murder of William Morgan, it would not of itself have sufficed to justify attaching even a suspicion to the entire institution of Freemasonry in the United States, or even to any considerable branch of it existing without the limits of the region where the events happened. Whatever might have been the private sentiments entertained of the danger attending the assumption of secret obligations, the exact nature of these was at the outset too little understood to sanction the inference that they allowed criminal enterprises. Extensive as the conspiracy against Morgan and Miller appeared to be, yet similar things have been done under the influence of passion, and in open and acknowledged violation of moral and religious duty, in all stages of the world's progress. It was hence no unreasonable thing to conclude that it might have happened once more. Censure was to be directed, if anywhere, against those overzealous members of the order who could be believed to have overstepped the bounds of reason and of justice, acknowledged as well by the law of the fraternity as by the higher one of God and of civil society. It was reserved for events coming somewhat later to develop the fact that in the instance of Morgan, Freemasons, so far from thinking themselves to be violating, were literally following the injunction which they felt to be laid upon them in their oaths. The law of Masonry was to them more than that of civil government or of the Deity, even when it was known directly to conflict with them. It was the truth of this proposition, slowly and gradually wrested from the lips of adhering members, that turned the current of popular indignation from the guilty individuals toward

the institution itself. It was the proof furnished of this
truth which created, the moral power of the political party
that soon sprung up in New York and Pennsylvania, and
that under the banner of opposition to all secret societies
rallied its tens of thousands in a fierce and vindictive, and
at times even a fanatical persecution of everything that
bore even the semblance of dreaded Freemasonry.)

It would be tedious to recapitulate all the particulars of
the evidence which ultimately fastened upon the public
mind a conviction of the reality of the proposition above
named. It may be sufficient to state the manner in which
the powerful efforts made to discover the guilty parties and
to bring them to justice were perpetually baffled. The
first and most natural impulse operating upon those who
united in an endeavor to maintain the law was to look to
the chief executive magistrate of New York for energetic
support. The person who held that office at the moment
was a no less distinguished man than the celebrated De
Witt Clinton. But he was at the same time a Freemason,
and what is more, he was high-priest of the General
Grand Chapter of the United States, in other words, the
highest officer of the order. The fact was known throughout the region of western New York, and was unquestionably relied upon as a protection from danger by those
who were concerned in the deeds of violence. Indeed it
afterward came out that what purported to be a letter
from him was freely used for the purpose of instigating
the members of the order to prosecute their schemes.
There are many living who yet suspect that the letter
was actually genuine ; but that suspicion is believed to be

unjust to the memory of the late Governor Clinton, who did what he could, as soon as he became apprized of the character of the offense, to bring the guilty to punishment. The fact, however, furnishes an instructive illustration of the great danger attending the existence of secret ties, which may even be suspected to conflict in the mind of a high officer of state with the performance of his public duties. The moral influence of his situation was thus wholly lost upon men who believed that, whatever he might say in public to the contrary, his sympathies were all with them; who supposed that his private obligations to conceal and never to reveal the secrets of his brother Masons, as well as to aid and assist in extricating them · from any difficulty in which they might become involved, might be depended upon, at least so far as to shelter them from the legal consequences of their own misdeeds, within the sphere of the executive influence. Was this an inference wholly unwarranted from the language of the Masonic oath? Let any impartial individual examine its nature, and answer affirmatively if he can. Doubtless De Witt Cliuton was wholly innocent of guilt, but his situation was not the less clearly one of conflict between his Masonic and his social and religious duty. Although he may have escaped contamination, another and weaker individual might have made himself accessory to the crime. At all events, it must be conceded that the situation in which he was thrown was one not unnaturally the consequence of his assumption of conflicting obliga-tions, and one in which no high civil officer under any government should ever be suffered to stand.

The second manifestation of the force of the Masonic obligation was made visible in the courts of justice, which are established to try persons charged with the commission of offenses against human life or liberty. The sheriffs, whose duty it was under the laws of New York to select and summon the grand-juries, were, in all the counties in which the deeds of violence against Morgan had been committed, Freemasons. Several of them had themselves been parties to the crime. They did not hesitate to make use of their power as officers of justice to screen the criminals from conviction. The jurors whom they summoned were most of them Masons, some of them participators in the offenses into which it became their civil duty to inquire. The consequence may readily be imagined. Money, time, and talent were expended in profusion, for the purpose of bringing the perpetrators of the crime complained of to condign punishment; but almost in vain. Some of the suspected persons were found and put upon their trial; but the secret obligation prevailed in the jury-box, and uniformly rescued them in the moment of their utmost need. Others vanished from the scene, and eluded pursuit even to the farthest limits of the United States. One man, and probably the most guilty, was tracked to the bosom of a lodge in the city of New York, by the members of which he was secreted, put on board of a vessel below the harbor, and dispatched to a foreign land. Five years were consumed in unavailing efforts to obtain a legal conviction of the various offenders. Nothing that deserves the name of a true verdict followed. Such a history of deeply-studied, skillfully-combined, and successfully-executed movements to set at naught the lawful-ly-constituted tribunals of justice, has at no other time been made evident in America. Important witnesses were carried off at the moment when their evidence was indispensable, and placed beyond the jurisdiction of the state ; or if present and interrogated, they stood doggedly mute ; or else they placed themselves entirely under the guidance of legal advisers employed to protect them from criminating themselves. It was made plain to the most ordinary capacity that the order was assuming the responsibility of the crime of some of its members. It was exerting itself to throw over the guilty the protecting garb of the innocent. The obligation of Freemasonry was then the law paramount, and the social system sunk into nothing by the side of it. Even distant lodges responded favorably to the call made upon them to aid in the defense of the endangered brethren, by actually voting and forwarding sums of money for their relief. And the brief and insignificant period of imprisonment which two or three of them paid as a penalty for comparatively light offenses, was spent by them in receiving the sympathy of a martyr's fate. The end of all was, that for the first time Masonry enjoyed its complete triumph. The men who actually participated in the murder have gradually dropped off, until it may be said that not a single individual remains within the United States. But they lived and died secure from every danger of legal punishment. The oath of Masonry came in conflict with the duty to society and to God, and succeeded in setting it aside.

The ends of justice were defeated; but the labors of those indefatigable persons who had striven day and night to promote them, were not altogether thrown away. The materials were collected to show the world the chain of connection wove by the Masonic obligations between the subordinate lodges of western New York and the higher authorities in the East. The popular attention was turned to every Masonic movement—not solely in the state in which had been the cause of offense, but in all of the neighboring states. Extraordinary powers to pursue the investigations to its source were demanded of various legislative bodies, and the treatment of these applications elicited the fact that Freemasonry exercised a power almost as great in the deliberative assemblies as in the executive council chamber, or in the jury-box of the courts. The opposition to Masonry became gradually more and more intensely political, and in the process took up an aspect of extreme and illiberal vindictiveness toward all who ventured to stay its progress. The other parties were compelled to bend to the force of the blast that was sweeping over them. The revelation made by Morgan, in the book which cost him his life, though at first called an imposture, proved on examination to be strictly true. But they embraced only the first three degrees of Masonry. Other persons, disgusted and indignant at the proceedings of their adhering brethren after the fate of Morgan was known to them, voluntarily came forward and supplied all the remaining forms used in America, and many of those which had been adopted in Europe. A considerable number openly and voluntarily seceded from the order.

A meeting of such persons held at Le Roy ended, as has been already stated, in a formal renunciation by them of all their obligations. Here and there in other states the example was followed by a few. There were more who silently seceded, having made up their minds never again to visit a lodge. Yet in spite of all this, in spite of the earnest exhortation addressed to his brethren by Colonel W. L. Stone, in a book written by him to prevail upon them to dissolve the lodges and chapters and to abandon Masonry altogether, it must be admitted that the great majority of the society remained equally unmoved by denunciation, flattery, or prayer. Some had the assurance publicly to deny the truth of all the allegations made against Masonry, and further to affirm that they had never taken obligations as Masons not compatible with their duties as citizens. Others—and the most important of these was Edward Livingston, then uniting with the possession of one of the chief posts of responsibility in the general government, that of the highest dignity in the Masonic hierarchy, made vacant by the death of Clinton, —deemed it the part of wisdom to remain sullenly dumb, abstaining from all controversy, and suffering the excitement against Masons to blow over and spend itself in vain. In this spirit Mr. Livingston proceeded to deliver what he called an Address to the General Grand Royal Arch Chapter of the United States, upon the occasion of his installation as general grand high-priest. He recommended that all attacks made upon the order to which they belonged should be met with dignified silence—as if dignified silence were not equally a resource for the

3

most atrocious criminal and for the most unspotted citizen.
The charge as against Mr. Livingston was surely worthy
of some little consideration when connected with the
evidence already laid before the public to sustain it.   It
was neither more nor less than this, that he, being secretary of state of the United States, one of the confidential
advisers of the president, and moreover the reputed author
of a strong proclamation issued by the chief-magistrate
against those in danger of falling into treasonable practices
by their connection with South Carolina nullification,
was yet himself under secret obligations which required
him to conceal the evidence of all the offenses denounced
in that state paper, provided only that it should be communicated to him under the seal of Masonic confidence.
Not to answer such a charge as this implied rather a
doubt of the ability to do so satisfactorily than a perfect
reliance upon the consciousness of innocence. If Masonry
was free from all the objections raised by its opponents,
what more effective step to establish its innocence than a
simple statement of the truth? If it was a valuable institution, worthy of preservation, surely the effort to
sustain it against injurious calumnies was worth making.
Could it be supposed that the unanimous testimony to the
alleged character of the oaths, brought by hundreds of
respectable persons who had taken them, but who now
renounce them, was to be discredited by the merely nega-
tive action of adhering Masons, however individually
respectable, or however exalted in position? Considering the precise nature of the difficulties by which they
were surrounded, it is clear that no defense could have

been assumed by them, in its character more nugatory. It manifested only the consciousness of wrong, combined with a dogged resolution never to admit nor to retract it.

The address of Mr. Livingston, such as it was, proved the inciting cause of the publication of a series of letters directed by Mr. Adams to him, which will be found to make a part of the present volume. In these papers the argument against the Masonic obligation, as the root of all the crimes committed in the case of Morgan, was pushed with a force which carried conviction to the minds of many persons at the time, and which seems even at this day scarcely to admit of reply. Mr. Livingston himself made no attempt at rejoinder. This was the part of discretion, for had he done so, there is little reason to doubt that Mr. Adams would have fulfilled his promise when he said to him, "Had you ventured to assume the defense of the Masonic oaths, obligations, and penalties; had you *presumed* to commit your name to the assertion that they can by any possibility be reconciled to the laws of morality, of Christianity, or of the land, I should have deemed it my duty to reply, and to have completed the demonstration before God and man that they *can not.*"

The opportunity for a complete and overwhelming victory was thus denied to Mr. Adams by the tacit secession from the field of Mr. Livingston. Yet the effect of his letters was by no means trifling in many states. The moral power of the opponents of Masonry visibly increased, and with it the earnestness of their political hostility to those who practiced its rites. It showed itself in the general election of state officers, both in New York and

Pennsylvania, and in the nomination of Mr. William Wirt as a candidate at the ensuing election for the presidency of the United States, in opposition to General Jackson, the incumbent, who was found to be a Freemason. Neither was Mr. Adams himself suffered to remain disconnected with the movement of political opinions upon the subject. A large convention of citizens of Massachusetts unanimously called upon him to suffer his name to be used in the canvass for the office of governor, which took place in that state in the year 1833. Reluctant as he was to enter into the arena, and to sacrifice his preference for the position in the House of Representatives of the United States, which he then occupied, the nature of the appeal made to him overcame all his scruples. The election took place. It terminated in the failure to make choice of any person by the requisite constitutional majority. The power of the party which had for a long time held the control of the government of Massachusetts, and with which Mr. Adams had up to this period co-operated, was broken under the effort to sustain Masonry against him. Had he determined to persevere, it is quite uncertain what might have been the consequences to the position of the commonwealth. But it was not his wish to press the matter beyond the point which a sense of duty dictated. No sooner was it ascertained by the return of the votes that a continuance of the contest in the legislature of the state was to be the result of his adherence to his position, than he determined to withdraw his name from the canvass. At the same time that he took this step, he caused to be published an address to the people of the common-

wealth, explaining his views of the connection between
Masonry and the politics of the country, and justifying
himself from the charges with which he had been most,
vehemently assailed. With this paper, the last in the
present volume, and the close of which is in a strain of
eloquence which alone should secure its preservation, Mr.
Adams appears to have terminated his public labors in
opposition to secret obligations and to Freemasonry. But
their effects were soon afterward made visible, by the
adoption of laws prohibiting the administration of extrajudicial oaths, by the voluntary dissolution of many of
the subordinate lodges, and by the tacit secession of a
large number of individual members. Indeed, such was the
silence preserved for a long time respecting the institution,
that its existence in Massachusetts might almost have been
questioned. The purposes for which the organized opposition had been made seemed so completely answered
that the motives for maintaining it were no longer strongly
felt. The current of public affairs soon afterward took a
new turn. Antimasonry gradually disappeared as an
agent to effect changes in the political aspect of the states,
and the individuals who had associated themselves in the
movement again joined the ordinary party organizations
with which they most nearly sympathized.

Thus it happened that Freemasonry, by cowering under
the storm, saved itself from the utter prostration which
would have followed perseverance in the policy of resistance. Years have passed away, and it again gives symptoms of revivification. A new and kindred institution
has suddenly manifested an extraordinary degree of

development under the guise of benevolence. What the precise nature of the obligations may be, which bind great numbers of citizens, mostly young, active men, into this connection, has not yet been fully brought to light. The objects are stated to be charity and the rendering of mutual aid. If these are all the purposes of the association, it can not be otherwise than meritorious. Yet it can scarcely be maintained that any unlimited pledge of secrecy is essential to the successful execution of them. In a republican form of government, the only real and proper fraternity is the system of civil society. To that every member is bound to bow. The obligations which it imposes neeb no veil of secrecy to cover them. Illustrated by the law of love enjoined by the superior authority of divine command, it marks out with distinctness to each individual the paramount duty of charity, of benevolence, and of mutual aid and support. There can be, therefore, no good excuse for resorting to smaller and narrower spheres for the invidious exercise of such virtues among those who ought to stand upon a perfectly even footing, when the broad and general one better answers to every useful and honorable exertion. The disadvantages attending the formation of all associations connected by secret obligations, no matter how harmless may be their appearance, are, first, that if they have any effect at all, it is injurious to those who do not choose to join them; secondly, that they substitute a private pledge of a doubtful nature to a few who have no moral right to the preference, for a clear and well-defined and entirely proper one given to the many. In all similar cases, the tendency to introduce objects of exertion in the smaller circle which conflict with those of society at large, and which may sometimes even threaten its safety, is obvious. It is the temptation presented to conspiracy which has made secret associations the objects of denunciation by the monarchs of Europe. The same thing should at all times render them marks for jealousy and distrust in republican states. They threaten the harmony of the community wherever they are. The pledge of political preference which was rapidly becoming ingrafted upon the Masonic institution in the United States, at the time of the Morgan excitement, and which had already produced visible results in many of the smaller towns of New York and New England, by unaccountably exalting some individuals to the depression of neighbors equally worthy, furnishes a good illustration of the mode in which social discord of the bitterest description may be made in the end to spring up. In view of the possibility of this hazard, it would seem as if few could be found, when once made sensible of the difficulty, willing deliberately to give occasion to it.

It is confidently believed that in the materials of the present volume will be found a solemn warning, conveyed by a voice in the feebleness of age still powerful over the sympathy of American citizens against the formation of secret obligations. As time rolls on its swift career, and as the generation which nursed the infant republic into strength disappears from the scene, the duty becomes stronger on those who succeed, to heed the counsels which its wisest and most experienced men leave behind them. The arguments of Mr. Adams, although directed against

the particular order of Freemasonry, will yet be found
susceptible of broader application, and extending themselves over all societies of which the radical error is, that
they shun the light of day. The pride of freemen—living
under a system of equal laws, with guaranties of the rights
of each individual—should be to sustain the junction of
innocence with liberty, the union of an open, honest heart
with an efficient and liberal hand. Such a state can not
co-exist with secret obligations. The person who lies under
an engagement which he must not reveal, whatever may
betide, can indeed be innocent and energetic, but he will
not be perfectly frank nor just to all men alike. Occasions may arise in which his fidelity to his private pledges
will come into conflict with his duty to society. Who is
then to decide for him what he must do? On either side
is moral difficulty and mental distress. If he betray his
associates, he spots his heart with violated faith. If he desert his country, he fails in a duty of even higher obligation.
The alternative is too painful to a conscientious spirit ever
knowingly to be hazarded with propriety. That such an
alternative is by no means impossible, who can doubt after
the cases of Eli Bruce, of De Witt Clinton, and of Edward
Livingston, in the Masonic history of the murder of Morgan? Much as he might regret it, what Freemason was
there in 1826 who did not perceive at a glance that his
pledge to his associates was to conceal the crime and to
shelter the criminal; while his duty to state and to heav-
en, to disclose the guilt and to denounce the author, was
written with a sunbeam on his heart? And how many
were there, who, instead of judging rightly of the relative

importance of the obligations, actually made themselves
accessories after the fact, by supplying the means of
escape from justice to their unworthy brethren? The
damning evidence of this truth must remain in the minds
of men as long as Masonry shall endure. It may indeed
be that other associations will spring up which may be
free from all the grossly objectionable engagements of that
institution. But who shall be secure against the intrusion
of evil when the portal stands invitingly open to its admission? Who shall be able to protect himself against the
designs of those of his associates to whom he has given a
secret control over his will? These are questions which
every citizen must answer for himself. It is with the
design that he may have at hand the means of acting
understandingly, that the present volume is put forth.
Young persons, who are especially liable to be carried
away by the fascination that always attends mystery, are
hereby furnished with an opportunity to weigh the arguments of a powerful remonstrant against any secret steps.
May they read, weigh, and deeply ponder the words of
wisdom, and may the effect of them be to preserve them
in the paths of liberty, of friendship, and of faith, early
marked out by their adviser as the guides of his own career,
unincumbered by obligations which they fear to disclose,
unembarrassed by promises which they know not how
conscientiously to perform!

MR. ADAMS' LETTERS

ON THE

MASONIC INSTITUTION.

Adams' Letters, Addresses, Etc.

TO A REVIEWER OF SHEPPARD'S DEFENSE OF THE MASONIC INSTITUTION.

The following letter from John Quincy Adams explains the views of his illustrious father, and of himself, on the subject of Freemasonry. It was written in reply to a note from our correspondent, who is reviewing Mr. Sheppard's *Defense of the Masonic Institution.* It may be recollected that Mr. Sheppard claimed the elder Adams as a patron of the order; and our correspondent took the liberty of addressing Mr. Adams, asking for information on this point. —*Boston Press.*

QUINCY, 22 August, 1831.

Sir:—The letter from my father to the Grand Lodge of Massachusetts, which Mr. Sheppard has thought proper to introduce into his address, was a *complimentary* answer to a friendly and patriotic address of the grand lodge to him. In it he expressly states that he had never been *initiated* in the order. He therefore knew nothing of their *secrets,* their *oaths,* nor their *penalties.* Far less had their practical operation been revealed by the

4

murder of William Morgan. Nor had the hand of the avenger of blood been arrested for five long years—and probably forever—by the contumacy of witnesses setting justice at defiance in her own sanctuary. Nor had the trial of an accomplice in guilt marked the influence of *one* juror under Masonic oaths upon the verdict of his eleven fellows.

That Mr. Sheppard should resort to a .etter from my father, a professedly uninitiated man, to liberate the Masonic institution from the unrefuted charge of unlawful *oaths*, of horrible and disgusting *penalties* and *secrets*, the divulging of which has been punished by a murder unsurpassed in human atrocity, is to me passing strange. All that my father knew of Masoury in 1798 was that it was *favorable to the support of civil authority;* and this he *inferred* from the characters of intitimate friends of his, and excellent men who had been members of the society. The inference was surely natural; but he had never seen the civil authority in conflict with Masonry itself. To speak of the Masonic institution as favorable to the support of civil authority at this day, and in this country, would be a mockery of the common sense and sensibility of mankind.

My father says he had known the love of the fine arts, the delight in hospitality, and the devotion to humanity of the Masonic fraternity. All these qualities, no doubt, then were, and yet are, conspicuous in many members of the society. They, and qualities of a yet higher order, were not less conspicuous in the Order of the Jesuits. They were conspicuous in many of the monastic orders—in the Inquisition itself, whose ministers in the very act of burning the body of the heretic to death were always actuated by the tenderest and most humane regard for the salvation of his soul.

The use of my father's name for the purposes to which Mr. Sheppard would now apply it is an injury to his memory, which I deem it my duty, as far as may be in my power, to redress. You observe he says he had never been *initiated* in the Masonic order. And I have more than once heard from his own lips *why* he had never enjoyed that *felicity.*

Mr. Jeremy Gridley, whom he mentions as having been his intimate friend, was grand master of the Massachusetts grand lodge. He was also the attorney-general of the Crown when, in October, 1758, my father, having finished his law studies and his school-keeping at Worcester, presented himself, a stranger, poor, friendless, and obscure, to ask of him the favor to present him to the superior court of the province, then sitting at Boston, for admission to the bar. Mr. Gridley, in his own office, examined the youthful aspirant with regard to his professional acquirements; gave him advice truly parental and dictated by the purest virtue; and then presented him to the court with a declaration that he had himself examined him, and could assure their honors that his legal acquirements were very considerable, and fully worthy of the admission which he solicited.

This kindness of Mr. Gridley was never forgotten by my father; I trust it never will be forgotten by his children. From that day forth, while Mr. Gridley lived, he was the intimate friend, personal and professional, of my father. He died in 1767. My father often resorted to him for friendly counsel, and, as he was grand master of the lodge, once asked his advice, whether it was worth his while to become a member of the society. In the candor of friendship Mr. Gridley answered him, *No,* adding that by aggregation to the society a young man might acquire a little artificial support, but that he did not need it, and that there was nothing in the Masonic institution worthy of his seeking to be associated with it.

So said at that time the Grand Master of the Massachusetts Masons, Jeremy Gridley; and such, I have repeatedly heard my father say, was the reason why he never joined the lodge.

The use of the name of Washington to give an

odor of sanctity to the institution as it now stands
exposed to the world is, in my opinion, as unwarrantable as that of my father's name.   On the
mortal side of human existence there is no name
for which I entertain a veneration more profound
than for that of Washington.   But he was never
called to consider the Masonic order in the light
in which it *must* now be viewed.   If he had been,
we have a pledge of what his conduct would have
been far more authoritative than the mere fact of
his having been a Mason can be in favor of the
brotherhood.*   If you wish to know what that
pledge is, please to consult the recently-published
writings of Thomas Jefferson, vol. I., from page
416 to 422; and especially the paragraph beginning at the middle of page 418.   I would earnestly recommend the perusal and meditation of the
whole passage to all virtuous and conscientious
Masons, of whom I know there are great numbers.

---

*Treating of the order of the Cincinnati,—a secret society composed
of soldiers of the Revolution,—Mr. Jefferson says: "The uneasiness
excited by this institution had very early caught the notice of General
Washington.   Still recollecting all the purity of the motives which
gave it birth, he became sensible that it might produce political evils,
which the warmth of those motives had masked.   Add to this, that it
was disapproved by the mass of citizens of the Union.   This alone was
reason strong enough in a country where the will of the majority is the
law, and ought to be the law.   He saw that the objects of the institution
were too light to be opposed to considerations as serious as these; and
that it was become necessary to annihilate it absolutely.   On this,
therefore, he was decided.   The first annual meeting at Philadelphia,

If they wish to draw precepts for their own conduct from the example and principles of Washington, or from the deliberate and anxious opinions and solicitude of Jefferson, they will find in those pages lessons of duty for themselves which they might consider it as presumption in me to offer them. The application of the principles in a case not identically the same, but in every essential point of argument similar, and in many respects from a weaker to a much stronger basis, I would leave to their own discretion, though first divested of its passions. It is, in my opinion, an unanswerable demonstration of the *duty* of every Mason in the United States at this day.

I never heard and do not believe that the Rev. Dr. Bently ever delivered or published a sermon censuring my father for anything he had ever said upon the subject of Masonry.

---

was now at hand. He went to that, determined to exert all his influence for its suppression. He proposed it to his fellow-officers, and urged it with all his powers. It met an opposition which was observed to cloud his face with an anxiety that the most distressful scenes of the war scarcely ever produced. It was canvassed for seven days, and, at length, it was no more a doubt what would be its ultimate fate. The order was on the point of receiving its annihilation by the vote of a great majority of its members." (Jefferson's Works, Vol. I. page 418.) Owing to the influence of French envoys,—who were greatly tinctured with infidelity, and filled with the spirit of Red Republicanism,—the society, contrary to the ardent wish of Washington, did not disband; but it *was* modified. Mr. Jefferson's conclusive reasons for disapproval of such institutions, are given in the succeeding pages of his works, and they are mostly equally applicable to all other secret orders.—[EDS.

The electoral vote of Massachusetts in 1801 *was* unanimous for my father.

You are at liberty to make what use of this letter you please, giving notice if you publish it that it is an answer to a letter of inquiry received by me.

I am, very respectfully, sir,

Your obedient servant,

JOHN QUINCY ADAMS.

TO EDWARD INGERSOLL, ESQ., PHILADELPHIA

[EXTRACT.]

September 21, 1831.

Mr. Chandler has truly informed you that I am a zealous Antimason,—to this extent: It is my deliberate opinion that from the time of the commission of the crimes committed at the kidnapping and murder of William Morgan, it became the solemn and sacred, civic and social duty of every Masonic lodge in the United States either to dissolve itself, or to discard forever all administration of oaths and penalties and all injunctions of secrecy of any kind to its members. I believed it also their duty, though of less imperious obligation, to abolish all their ill-assorted, honorific titles, and childish or ridiculous pageants.

I believed it also a duty sacredly incumbent upon every individual Freemason in the United States to use all the influence in his power to prevail upon his brethren of the order to the same end, that is, to the total abolition of the order, or to its discarding forever all oaths, all penalties, all secrets, and all fantastic titles, exhibitions, and ceremonies heretofore used in the institution.

Believing these to be their duties I did not feel myself called to take an active part in the controversy which I saw arising in the community concerning them. I took considerable pains to avoid entering into that controversy. I endured from individuals of the fraternity, instigated from the passions of the order, falsehood, by statements in their newspapers'that I was one of their members; *perjury*, to affect the presidential election, by an affidavit sworn to before a Masonic magistrate by a Master Mason that he had sat with me twice at meetings of a lodge at Pittsfield; insulting, cajoling, threatening anonymous letters from Masonic sources; abusive slander and vituperation in Masonic newspapers, pamphlets, and even volumes; and other wrongs of which it behooves me not to speak. All these I have endured for a space now of at least four years, without reply, without complaint, never disguising in the conversation of social intercourse the opinions above expressed;

never seeking occasion to promulge them; and
declining time after time, on many occasions and
in various forms, to engage in the turmoil of Masonic and Antimasonic warfare. At last an English shepherd of Masonic sheep at Wiscasset, in
Maine, has the impudence to vouch in my father
as a witness to the sublime and transcendent virtues of Masonry, and in the same pamphlet casts
a due portion of his Masonic filth at me; for
what? Because in a confidential letter, not intended for the public, and published without my
consent, I had once written that I should never
be a Mason; and because I had twice, by special
invitation, been present as a mere spectator at
meetings of Antimasons in Boston. Still I should
have overlooked Mr. Sheppard and his Masonic
virtues, with the rest, but that the editor of the
Boston Press, undertaking to review his defense
of Masonry, wrote to me to inquire what I knew
of this pretended panegyric upon Masonry by my
father. I then wrote the letter which you have
seen, and which the friendly commentary of Mr.
Walsh—to whom you may, if you please, with my
compliments, show this letter—attributes to the
" *error of the moon.*"

I said, " the *crimes* committed at the kidnapping
and murder of William Morgan." Do you know
what they were? Were they not,

1.   Fraudulent abuse in repeated forms of the process of the law to obtain, upon false pretenses, possession of the person of Morgan.

2.   Infamous slander in those false pretenses by first arresting him on a charge against him of petty larceny.

3.   Previous slander in newspaper advertisements denouncing him as a swindler and impostor, calling upon *brethren* and *companions* particularly to observe, mark, and *govern themselves accordingly*, and declaring that the *fraternity* had amply provided against his evil designs.

4.   Conspiracy of Masonic lodges assembled in great numbers, *per fas et nefas*, by the commission of *any* crime to suppress his book.   .

5.   Arson, by setting fire at night to Miller's printing-office, in which building were eight or ten persons asleep, whose lives were saved only by the early discovery of the projected conflagration.

6.   Fraud, deception, and treachery in procuring from Morgan himself a part of his manuscript, which was finally sent by a special messenger to the General *Grand Chapter* of the United States in session at New York.

7.   Kidnapping, – too successfully practiced upon Morgan,—attempted upon Miller.

8.   False imprisonment and transportation of

Morgan beyond the bounds of the United States into a foreign territory.

9. A murder, taking nine days in its perpetration, keeping the wretched and helpless victim throughout the whole of that time in a state of continual and cruel torture.

Sleep upon this list of peccadilloes, and to-morrow I will give you upon them a word of comment.   Yours,

JOHN QUINCY ADAMS.

TO EDWARD INGERSOLL, ESQ.

QUINCY, September 22, 1831.

Dear Sir:—I gave you in my last letter a list of *nine* crimes, among the most atrocious that can be perpetrated by human agency, committed in the original transactions connected with what has been, by an exceedingly inappropriate euphony called, the *abduction* and murder of William Morgan. *Abduction* is a word of lamb-like innocence compared with the ingredients of wickedness which composed the crime of his taking off. Language sinks under the effort to express its complicated malignity.

These crimes I allege were committed by *the fraternity.* They were instigated by no impulse

of individual passions,—by none of the stimulants
to the ordinary outrages of man upon man,—by no
personal animosity,—by no purpose of robbery.
They were the crimes of *the craft*, of which the
guilty agents by whom they were consummated
were but the fanatical instruments.

And here I pray you to remark that I have stated these crimes interrogatively. I have inquired
of you whether they were *not* the crimes committed in those transactions, to the end that if you
find upon inquiry that I have set them down in-
correctly or with exaggeration, you may reduce
them in number or in virulence to their just and
well-proportioned standard.

I charge them upon *the craft* as *the means* by
which public notice had been given beforehand
that the fraternity had amply provided against his
designs.

In these crimes several hundreds of persons appear to have participated, as principals or accessories, before or after the fact. The measures
were taken not individually, but as results of corporate deliberation in sundry lodges.

Mr. Miner, one of the most amiable and benevolent of men, has mistaken the terms of the Antimasonic proposition. There are no doubt degrees
of exasperation of different temperature among
the Antimasons: but I know of none disposed to

hold every individual Mason responsible for the tragedy of Morgan's murder. All know that there are now, as there always have been, Masons among the most respectable and virtuous members of the community. But they belong to a vicious institution, and it is their duty to withdraw from that institution, to abolish it, or to purify it from its vices, oaths, penalties, and secrets.

That the institution is vicious might be very conclusively inferred from the effects disclosed in the nine crimes above enumerated, even if their causes were yet secret. But those causes have been divulged. We know that every Entered Apprentice of Masonry has, hoodwinked and with a halter round his neck, administered to him an oath, the words of which he is required to repeat with his lips, never to divulge the secrets of the order, and binding himself by "*no less a penalty* than to have his throat cut across, his tongue torn out by the roots, and his body buried in the rough sands of the sea at low-water mark, where the tide ebbs and flows twice in twenty-four hours." Morgan divulged these secrets, and his fate is the practical commentary upon the penalty.

The oath, the penalty, the secret, and Morgan's corpse at the bottom of Niagara River, where a shrewd brother of the craft "guessed he would

publish no more books," are illustrations of each
other which it would take much sophistry to obscure, much prevarication to confuse. Mr. Miner
has taken this oath, and bound himself by no less
than this penalty. It is wise and prudent in him
therefore not to violate the oath; and he would
assuredly not have been the man to execute the
penalty upon Morgan for considering it a dead
letter.

But will Mr. Miner tell you that the penalty is,
or that it is not, a dead letter? If it is, surely the
oath is the same, and then it is mere profanity;
a taking of the name of God in vain; odious in
proportion to the disgusting solemnity of the form
n which it is administered. If it is not a dead
letter, what is it? Some of the Masonic *defenses*
allege that it is only an imprecation—"under no
less a *penalty* than *to have my throat cut*"—a mere
imprecation! Is it not then a paltering with
words in double senses? A penalty is not an imprecation, and to have the throat cut across, and
the tongue torn out by the roots, is not expulsion
from a lodge. The substance of the defense is
that the penalty is a *brutum fulmen;* that there is
no authority existing in or conferred by the institution to carry it into execution; and that it is a
special *charge* to all Masons upon their admission
to observe faithfully the laws of God and of the

land. But for every degree of Masonry there is a
separate oath and a diversified penalty; and in
some of the higher degrees it includes a promise
to carry into effect the punishments of the fraternity. I have heard of the instructions from
the owner of a piratical cruiser to his captain, directing him to take, burn, sink, or destroy any
merchant vessel of any nation that might fall in
his way, and to dispose of the people on board of
them so as that they might not prove afterwards
troublesome; but to be specially careful not to in-
fringe upon the laws of nations or of humanity.
This man must have been a Mason of at least the
Royal Arch degree.

That the oaths and penalties of Masonry were
not understood by the multitudes of Masons accessory to the commission of the nine crimes
enumerated in my list as mere imprecations is
self-evident. By them they were understood according to their plain, unambiguous import, as an
absolute, unequivocal forfeiture of *life,* and an explicit consent of the person taking the oath that
he should be put to death in the horrid manner
described in the terms of the penalty if he should
divulge the secrets of the order. But whether the
penalty be, as it purports, a real penalty, or a
mere imprecation, will Mr. Miner say that it is a
form of words and obligations fit to be adminis-

tered with a solemn invocation of the name of
God to a Christian and a freeman?   Cruel and
unusual punishments are equally abhorrent to the
mild spirit of Christianity, and to the spirit of
equal liberty.   The infliction of them is expressly
prohibited in the Bill of Rights of this Commonwealth, and yet thousands of her citizens have attested the name of God to subject themselves to
death by tortures which cannibal savages would
instinctively shrink from inflicting.

It has therefore been, in my opinion, ever since
the disclosure of the Morgan murder crimes, and
of the Masonic oaths and penalties by which they
were instigated, the indispensable duty of the Masonic order in the United States, either to dissolve
itself, or to discard forever from its constitution
and laws all *oaths*, all *penalties*, all *secrets;* and, as
ridiculous appendages to them, all *mysteries* and
pageants.   Believing this to be the duty of the
whole order, I have deemed it a duty equally indispensable of every individual Mason to use in
calmness and moderation all his influence with
the fraternity to come to one or the other of these
results.   And I have, since the New York elections of the last autumn, deemed this to be a duty
especially and above all incumbent upon Mr. Clay.
I mean that he should have set a similar example
to that of Washington, in endeavoring to prevail

upon the Order of the Cincinnati to dissolve themselves, or at least to discard the most exceptionable parts of their constitution, in which latter
purpose he succeeded. I have not said this to Mr.
Clay because in the estimate of his duties he must
be his own counsellor, and I know he has had advice from another quarter, which he has doubtless
deliberately weighed. But it brings me to a point
upon which I shall ask a few minutes further of
your patience for your friend hereafter.

JOHN QUINCY ADAMS.

TO EDWARD INGERSOLL, ESQ.

QUINCY, 23 September, 1831.

Dear Sir:—From the nature of the Masonic
oaths, penalties, and secrets, and the construction
given to them—not a forced and unnatural one,
but conformable to the plain import of their terms
—by multitudes of Masons in the western part of
New York, the crimes immediately connected
with the murder of Wm. Morgan were committed. I charge them therefore upon the institution; and if Masonry had been until then a perfectly innocent and even useful institution, from
the time of the commission of those crimes it
would have ceased to be so. From that time the

5

community acquired the right of calling upon the fraternity to discontinue and renounce at least the administration of oaths, the imposition of all forms of penalties, and all secrets whatever.

A large and increasing portion of the community have made this demand,—a demand just and reasonable in itself, and the more so as the oaths, penalties, and secrets have been divulged, not only by Morgan's book, but by the concurring testimony of numerous seceding Masons. The oaths, the penalties, and the secrets—whether all disclosed with perfect accuracy or not, whether understood as they were by the murderers of Morgan or as explained by the defenders of Masonry,—are unreasonable, odious, and, I believe, unlawful. The oaths of all Masons heretofore admitted, if they ever had any binding force, are dissolved by the fact of the public disclosure of the secrets which they had bound themselves to keep. Their country calls upon them to disclaim henceforth and forever all secrets, and as incidental to the injunction of them, all oaths and penalties. This reasonable and moderate call has not only been resisted by the great body of Freemasons throughout the United States, but no man, high or low, eminent or obscure, has dared to avow this opinion and unite in this call without being assailed in his reputation, robbed of his good name, in sulted, abused, and vilified openly and in secret, by individual Masons, and by organized lodges, a body of at least two hundred thousand men scattered over the whole Union—all active and voting men, linked together by secret ties for purposes of indefinite extent; bound together by oaths and penalties operating with terrific energy upon the imagination of the human heart and upon its fears; embracing within the penalty of its laws the president of the United States and his leading competitors ; and winding itself round every great political party for support, like poisonous ivy round a sturdy oak, and round every object of its aversion like the boa-constrictor round its victim. Such in faint and diluted colors is at this time the image of the Masonic institution in these United States. Commanding despotically a large portion of the public press, intimidating by its terrors multitudes of others, and amid all its internal dissensions uniting with the whole mass of its power against every common adversary, one of the most alarming and pernicious characters in which it now presents itself, is that of its political dominion. You tell me that you are Antimasonic in your opinions and feelings, but are perplexed by the mixture of politics with Antimasonry. But you place herein the effect before the cause. The mixture of politics is with Masonry. It is

the misfortune of Mr. Clay to be entangled with
Masonry, and I sincerely regret that he has not
felt it his duty, as I think it was, to shake off his
shackles.   His motives, I have no doubt, were
generous, but the effect is that *he* sustains and
identifies himself with the Masonic cause.   That
cause is now sustained *only* by such artificial and
unnatural pillars.   Neither Mr. Clay nor you (for-
give me for saying) estimate at its true value the
cause of Antimasonry.   You look chiefly to the
motive of its supporters, and distrust them too
much.

You ask if *Masonry* should be made answerable
for the crimes of a few individual Masons.   Should
the royal government of Rome have been abolished for the violence committed upon a single
woman?   Should the decemvirate have been sub-
verted for the murder of Virginia by her own
father?   Should the tribe of Benjamin have been
exterminated for the brutal abuse of one Levite's
concubine?   Should the British nation have gone
to war with Spain for the cutting off by a few
Spaniards of one smuggler's ears?   In all those
cases, and in numberless others which swarm in
human history, the connection between the crime
and the institution made answerable for it was in-
finitely more remote than the cluster of Morgan
murder crimes is from the vitals of Masonry.   But

I have spoken only of the crimes committed at the time. Look at the government of the State of New York, struggling in vain from that time to this,—five long years,—to bring the perpetrators of the murder to punishment. See judges, sheriffs, witnesses, jurors, entangled in the net of Masonry, and justice prostrated in her own temple by the touch of her invisible hand. Several of the *"abductors"* have indeed been convicted, and among them one sheriff of a county. Three or four upon their own confession of guilt. You say you " have been told by men who care much more for truth than for Masonry that there is no reason to believe that any Mason has refused to give testimony on account of Masonic obligations." My dear sir, go to the records of the courts. You will find witnesses refusing to testify upon the express ground of Masonic obligations, avowing that they consider those obligations paramount to the laws of the land. You will see them contumacious to the decisions of the court, fined and imprisoned for contempt, suffer the punishment ather than bear the testimony, and, instead of expulsion, be refunded, at least in part, for their fines by contributions from the lodges. I give you names: Isaac Allen, Eli Bruce, Ezekiel Jewett, John Whitney, Orsamus Turner, Erastus Day, Sylvanus Cone, Elisha M. Forbes, Benjamin Enos.

You will find much more. You will find Masonic grand and petit juries, summoned by Masonic sheriffs, eager to sit upon the trials, perverting truth and justice when admitted on the array, and often excluded upon challenge to the favor; and last of all, you will find one of the men most deeply implicated in the murder, screened from conviction by *one* Mason upon his jury.

"It is not and it can not come to good."

That this enormous train of abuses should be sustained by those who have it in abhorrence, and that every individual denouncing it should be hunted down as if he himself were a pest to society, because Masonry has fastened itself to the skirts both of General Jackson and Mr. Clay, to sink or swim with them, is itself one of the most objectionable properties of the institution. Clay Masonry has become not only the familiar denomination of a great political party, but of a party which, to put down a high, pure, and virtuous manifestation of popular sensibility, takes to its bosom Jacksonism itself. So it was in all the New York elections of last November. So it has been in the elections of the last Massachusetts legislature. Clay Masons gave New York to the Regency to put down the Antimason Granger. Clay Masons made a Jackson man a senator for our county of Plymouth over a National Republican, with three hundred more popular votes, because, forsooth, he was the Antimasonic and his competitor the *Masonic* candidate. And yet I hear Masons complain of proscription and disfranchisement.

I may, perhaps, publish part of these letters, but without at all implicating you. Show them, if you please, to Mr. Walsh, as the moon-struck visions of your friend.

JOHN QUINCY ADAMS.

TO EDWARD INGERSOLL, ESQ.

QUINCY, 22 October, 1831.

Dear Sir:—One month has elapsed since, in answer to some remarks in a friendly letter from you on the subject of Masonry and its antidote, I gave you with freedom and candor my sentiments concerning them, and a view of the progressive steps by which I had been reluctantly drawn into a public participation in this controversy. I authorized you to show my letters to Mr. Walsh, because having long been with me upon terms of private friendship and of personal confidence, he had denounced me to the public as a madman (upon this subject) for a letter written and pub-

lished in vindication of my father's reputation
from Masonic slander. I had no expectation of
converting Mr. Walsh, though I did hope that
this mode of noticing the severity of his censure
might awaken a sentiment of kindness in his mind,
which either had departed or was slumbering
when he consigned me to the jurisdiction of the
moon. He since has made me more than amends
by his notice of my eulogy upon Mr. Monroe,
and, as I have always been a friend of toleration
in politics as well as in religion, I must compromise for being considered by him a lunatic upon
Masonry and the Hartford Convention, in consideration of an over-allowance of merit upon points
on which his opinions concur with mine.

Within that month events in relation to the
Masonic controversy have occurred of no trifling
magnitude. That Mr. Walsh and Mr. Sargeant
consider Antimasonry as yet a subject for *scorn*
certainly staggers my faith in the correctness of
my own impressions. A very sincere respect for
their opinions calls upon me for a severe review
of my own, and makes me feel with double force
the admonition, in your kind letter of the 17th
instant, to be specially cautious of error and exag
geration in anything that I may say on this score
to the public. It was indeed under that conviction that I submitted to you *interrogatively* the list

of nine atrocious crimes committed, as I believed, in connection with the murder of William Morgan, and which I charged upon the Masonic institution. If mistaken either in the number or aggravation of the crimes, or in the *principle* of imputing them to the institution, I was desirous of being corrected by your enlightened judgment and more accurate information. I am, therefore, happy to learn that Mr. Miner will reply to my letters *in full*. But he is the last man in the world with whom I would willingly have a controversy. I am perfectly willing to publish in his *Village Record* that portion of my letters to you which I shall ultimately conclude to publish at all; but before that I wish to have the benefit of your corrections as well in point of fact as of principle, derivable from the inquiries which at my suggestion you have made. I should also be glad to know if Mr. Miner or you yourself would be willing to have your names in the publication; you, as the person to whom the letters were addressed; he, as the person referred to in them. In naming him it did not occur to me that he would see the letters; but I fully approve of your course in showing them to him, and also to the other persons whom you have mentioned. From the nature of the controversy, and precisely because Masonic warfare is secret, I have determined to publish

nothing against Masonry but under the responsibility of my *name*. I have no right, however, to
take the same liberty with the names of others,
and shall carefully avoid using them without permission or special justifying reason.

The nomination of Messrs. Wirt and Ellmaker
at Baltimore is one of those prominent events
which have occurred since my last letters to you
were written. Mr. Miner has sent me a copy of
a printed hand-bill addressed to the citizens of
Chester County, signed by himself and seventeen
other Masons, heading a republication of Mr.
Wirt's letter to the convention at Baltimore, and
declaring their concurrence in every word and
sentiment of that letter. But that letter most
distinctly declares Mr. Wirt's approbation both
of the *end* and the *means* of the Antimasons; the
end being the abolition of Freemasonry, and the
means the ballot-box against all *adhering* Masons
and all neutrals. What part of my charges, then,
does Mr. Miner mean to contest?

The declarations of General Peter B. Porter
and W. B. Rochester have also been made public
since the date of my letters to you. What is
there in my charges that is not fully sanctioned
by them? They unequivocally advise the surrender of the charters. They say Mr. Clay thinks
with them. Why has Mr. Clay refused to say so?

Delicacy? Has Mr. Clay ever considered it a matter of delicacy for a candidate to give pledges of his opinions upon controverted points of political interest? Does Mr. Clay *scorn* Antimasonry, like Mr. Walsh and Mr. Sargeant? If he does, it is evident General P. B. Porter and W. B. Rochester do not.

I am happy to find *you* do not. Mr. Wirt frankly tells the Baltimore convention that until two or three days before they met he had considered *Antimasonry* as a *farce*, and wondered how such an excitement should have been blown up from what he thought so trifling a cause. He scorned Antimasonry. Why? Because he knew nothing of the facts, and believed Masonic misrepresentations. The moment the facts were disclosed to him, or rather the moment he could bring himself to turn his face to them, the scales fell from his eyes,—he approves the *end* of the Antimasons, and he approves their *means*. His case is the case of thousands and tens of thousands. Yet Mr. Wirt had sworn to keep the secrets of Masonry upon no less a penalty than the fate of Morgan. He had forgotten the secret, and perhaps the oath. How such a man as Mr. Wirt could ever have taken such an oath and then forgotten it, is among the inscrutables and unaccountables of human conduct

The Antimasons of this commonwealth have nominated Samuel Lathrop for governor in the place of Mr. Lincoln. They first did me the honor to nominate me, but I declined. Governor Lincoln is my personal friend, and I approve of his administration in general. I regretted that they did not nominate him. No answer accepting this nomination has yet appeared from Mr. Lathrop. Mr. Lincoln will at all events be re-elected, for there is not a state in the Union where Masonry is so strong as in this; and the Masons will support Lincoln, though his answer to the Antimasonic Committee is as severe against Masonry as anything I have ever said or written. But there was something in his remarks upon Antimasonry which they took for scorn— though I did not. Their candidate is a man of excellent character, a warm Federalist, and heretofore *the* Federal candidate for governor.

The State of Vermont is now purely Antimasonic in all its branches, with a governor, council, and majority of the House of Representatives, elected as Antimasons against both Clay and Jackson Masonry. Vermont is the first state where this victory has been achieved. Yet it was not there that Morgan was murdered.

I shall expect somewhat anxiously your exposition of facts conflicting with my statements. I know Mr. Stone, of the New York *Commercial,* believes that the kidnappers of Morgan did not at first *intend* to murder him. Perhaps he believes that the arrest of him for petty larceny was not connected with the project to kidnap him. I know too well that he dwells much upon the alleged baseness of Morgan's moral character. I set the question of his character aside; but a charge of *theft* against a man for neglecting to return a borrowed shirt—what chance has character against slander like that?

Very respectfully, your friend,
JOHN QUINCY ADAMS.

TO WILLIAM H. SEWARD, ESQ., AUBURN, N. Y.

QUINCY, 17 October, 1831.

Dear Sir:—Your letter from Boston of September 15th was duly received, and not immediately answered, chiefly from a doubt as to where to address a letter which would reach you without delay at that time.

The nomination of candidates for the next election of president and vice-president of the United States by a unanimous vote, relieved me from the only apprehension I had previously entertained,—that the convention at Baltimore would not be able to agree in their choice.

Much now depends—for the cause of Antimasonry, perhaps everything depends—upon the course pursued by the party in the approaching elections in the State of New York. I learn that in those of Pennsylvania the present year will indicate rather a falling off from the cause, though no real defection of its supporters. In this commonwealth the result may be the same. I shall regret this, because the more attentively I have observed the character of the Masonic institution as it *now* exists in the United States the more thoroughly I am convinced that it is the greatest political evil with which we are now afflicted.

The Antimasons in this state have concluded to support a candidate against the present governor, much to my regret. They did me the honor to nominate me, but I felt it my duty to decline the offer. They have nominated Samuel Lathrop, but it is doubted whether he will accept. The opinions of the present governor are very decidedly against Masonry, and the opposition to him will deter many from joining the Antimasons who would otherwise have voted with them.

I pray your acceptance of the within eulogy upon James Monroe, and I am,

Very respectfully, dear sir,

Your obedient servant,

JOHN QUINCY ADAMS.

TO RICHARD RUSH, ESQ., YORK, PENN.

[EXTRACT.]

QUINCY, 25 October, 1831.

The Masonic and Antimasonic controversy drags along,—deepening, widening, embittering, as it proceeds. In proportion as the popular excitement against Masonry spreads, the Masons close their ranks and rally round their hideous idol. Of the Antimasons, I wish that the discretion and the plain dealing and consistency were equal to the goodness of their cause. I can not absolutely say they are not; but I do not understand some of their recent movements, and must wait to see their consequences before passing judgment upon them. It has been circulated by some of them here, as it was stated to you, that I had suggested to them the name of Mr. Wirt for their nomination at Baltimore; but it is not so. I much prefer the nomination of Mr. Wirt to that of Mr. McLean, which I fully expected; but of the proceedings at Baltimore there are rumors circulated by the Masonic party which I hope are without foundation. It is said, among other things, that the convention was as equally divided between Mr. Wirt and Mr. McLean as forty-one to thirty-eight, and that it is very doubtful whether the party will sustain the nomination of their convention. Here an Antimasonic convention did me the honor to nominate me for the office of governor of this commonwealth, but I felt it my duty to decline the nomination. They then nominated Samuel Lathrop, a very worthy man, but it is said that without declining their nomination, he has answered that he is and will be a strong supporter of Mr. Clay for the presidency. They have not yet published either my answer or Mr. Lathrop's.

About a month since, Edward Ingersoll made in a letter to me some remarks upon this controversy, in answer to which I wrote him three letters, part of which I informed him I might probably publish. I charged in the form of interrogations *nine* specific atrocious crimes in the transactions connected with the murder of William Morgan, independent of all the subsequent judicial prevarications, contumacies, and perjuries. I charged them not upon all individual Masons, but upon the Masonic institution,—upon its *oaths, penalties,* and *secrets ;* and I asked him if my list of crimes were overcharged in number or measure to reduce them to the standard of truth; and if they were not chargeable upon *Masonry,*

to answer the reasons which I gave him for so
considering them. Mr. Ingersoll, who avows
himself Antimasonic in principle and feeling, has
shown my letters to several persons, and among
the rest to our friend Miner, who I understand
has undertaken to reply to my letters in full. I
learn further that your grand lodge or grand
chapter are about to enter upon the arena and
make a powerful *defense* of Masonry. A principal object of my letters to Ingersoll was to *bring
out* the Masons upon the Morgan-murder crimes
Their tactics hitherto have been to smuggle them
out of sight. Sheppard's *Defense* speaks of the
murder itself as *doubtful,* and styles it as a mere
drunken scrape at which Masons were present. The
formal defense of Masonry by the grand lodge of
Rhode Island says they can not tell whether Morgan was or was not murdered, for that *they know
nothing about it.* So effectually have they, by
their management of the press, kept those transactions out of view that thousands and thousands,
like Mr. Wirt, have gone on year after year
scorning and laughing at Antimasonry as a farce,
and thinking Masonry a Sir Roger de Coverly
Club, because they could not *look at the facts.* My
interrogatory specification of an Anti-Parnassus
of crimes was intended to bring the Masons to an
issue upon the fact and law, fairly out before the

tribunal of the public. I have promised that if I
do publish any part of my letters to Ingersoll
they shall first appear in Mr. Miner's *Village
Record*. Miner himself will reply to them, and
between him and me I shall be content to stand
alone; but if the grand lodge or grand chapter
of Pennsylvania come down upon me, especially
during the session of congress, I shall want
auxiliary force, and hope you will be in the field
again.

Vermont is now completely Antimasonic, because, from their proximity to the Morgan murder, the facts have forced themselves upon the
public eye in spite of all Masonic suppressions.
The letters of General Peter B. Porter and W. B.
Rochester give a foreboding of the prospects of
the New York elections now at hand. There is
danger of a falling off in this state, owing to the
Antimasonic nomination against Governor Lincoln

                Ever faithfully yours,
                        JOHN QUINCY ADAMS.

TO HIS EXCELLENCY, LEVI LINCOLN, GOVERNOR
OF MASSACHUSETTS.

[EXTRACT.]

WASHINGTON, 18 December, 1831

My Dear Sir :—I can not forbear immediately
to acknowledge the receipt of your two kind
letters of the 11th and 12th instants, although a
heavy and quite unexpected burden of occupa-
tion, imposed upon me by the duties of the
station in which I fear I have rashly permitted
myself to be placed, will deprive me of the
opportunity of which I *did* propose to avail myself of communicating with you upon one topic
especially of transcendent interest to my mind.
I mean neither more nor less than the institution
of Freemasonry in these United States.

The speaker of the House of Representatives
of the United States has thought proper to appoint me chairman of the Committee of Manu-
factures,—a station from which I have in vain
endeavored to obtain a release. It will leave me
little time for anything else, and particularly not
for the review, which it was my purpose to
take of the Masonic controversy now in progress in our own and the neighboring states, and

which I believe destined to produce consequences
deeply affecting the interests, the happiness, and
the liberties of our country.

The design must for the present be postponed,
and perhaps my undertaking would, at all events,
have been premature. It is now a little more
than five years since the true character of *Free-masonry*, as existing in this Union, was disclosed
to the public eye. It first exploded by the catas-
trophe of one of the deepest tragedies that ever
was enacted upon the scene of human being,
exploded by a complication of nine or ten of the
most atrocious crimes that ever were conceived in
human hearts or committed by human hands,—
crimes committed not by men in the stations of
life to which ignorance is a snare, intemperance a
stimulant, or indigence a temptation,—not by
men under the instigations of malice or revenge,—but by men in the educated classes of
society; men who had been instructed in the
duties of Christians and citizens; men above the
pressure of want; men, in other respects and
independent of their secret and mystical ties to
this institution, of fair and respectable lives;
men enjoying the confidence of their fellow-citizens, and holding offices of trust committed to
them by that confidence.

We see these men, not in the solitary depravity

of a single heart, but after repeated consultation in lodges and chapters, combined, and for the commission of more than one of the crimes, abusing the sacred authority of the law with which they had been invested for the furtherance and execution of justice, to the commission of swindling, slander, theft, false imprisonment, man-stealing, treachery, arson, transportation of a citizen beyond the limits of his country, and to close the catalogue, *foul and midnight murder.*

Such was the first disclosure of the *secrets* of Freemasonry,—such was the practical exposition of its laws. The laws themselves were afterward revealed. It was to prevent the revelation of them that all these crimes were committed, and, by the retributive justice of Providence, it was the very commission of the crimes which brought the laws to light.

It is not then to Freemasonry as a *secret society,* of mysteriously concerted operation and portentous power; of strangely mingled royal and priestly titles with fantastical fooleries of attire and pageantry; **of** ostentatious devotion and hidden carousals; of charity and of revelry in the proportion of Sir John Falstaff's tavern bill for bread and for sack,—it is not to this society, such as it was before the murder of William Morgan, that I intended to entreat your attention as a citizen, a Christian, a magistrate, and a man. Freemasonry, as known to the world before the commission of the Morgan-murder crimes, might not be worthy of your attention. From the time when the crimes were committed, and the laws by which they were committed were revealed, that a citizen of the United States should exist,. who can ask himself, " What is this to me ? " is as unaccountable as the fascinations of Freemasonry itself.

But the disclosure of the crimes and the disclosure of the laws were not enough. Five years has the government of New York been struggling, not as it ought instantly to have done, to strangle this hydra with unnumbered heads, but to execute upon the criminals a feeble and ineffectual justice; five years, in the face of this nation, have Masonic sheriffs, jurors, and witnesses betrayed their duty to their country and their God, to screen the guilty from punishment; five years have lodges, chapters, and encampments aided and abetted in the concealment of the crimes and in the escape of the criminals from justice, while a gang of two hundred thousand Masons, from every nook and corner of the Union, are joining in one concerted yell of persecution ! persecution ! and certifying and swearing that *they* never took an oath incompatible with their duty to their religion or the laws of the land. "*In generalibus latet dolus*" was the maxim of the old logicians. The denial of the Royal Arch oath is a miserable prevarication. The Entered Apprentice's oath and penalty is itself a violation of all religion and of the constitution of our commonwealth. To say that such an oath is not to affect religion or politics, is to unite impossibilities. It is to take a firebrand in the hand, by thinking of the frosty Caucasus. The four Royal Arch Masons who sunk Morgan's body in the Niagara River inflicted upon him the penalty of the Entered Apprentice's oath. Their names are known probably to every lodge in the State of New York, but they can not be convicted, for none will testify, and the grand chapter at New York which has the power of expulsion throughout the state, so far from expelling any one of the kidnappers or murderers of Morgan, has aided them with money to support them in prison and to pay their fines. But I must abridge this letter. From the combined consideration of these three elements,—

1. The practical disclosure of the character and laws of Masonry by the Morgan-murder crimes.

2. From the subsequent disclosure of its written laws, oaths, and penalties in literal conformity

and obedience, to which these crimes were committed.

3. From the struggle of five years' duration between the government of New York to bring these crimes to punishment, and the successful Masonic combination to defeat the law of the land and to screen the guilty from its power.

From these combined considerations there appear to me to result solemn and sacred duties to every citizen of the Union, and especially to every citizen invested with authority. It was therefore that I commenced this correspondence by the inquiry whether you were acquainted with the facts. They are known to few. I find by your answer that some of them, not important, are still unknown to you. The extent of the combination, preceding the murder of Morgan, is even now known only to the surviving accomplices in the guilt. Of the four immediate perpetrators of the murder, one may yet reveal the horrid tale, the minute particulars of which are known to many *worthy* brothers of the craft. Much of Masonic participation, both before and after the fact, will probably never be known abroad from the recesses of the lodge. With these observations I have mingled no reference whatever to the Antimasonic party, their proceedings or their leaders. I look only to their *cause;* and if that is under bad management, I can only express the hope that it may be more energetically taken into their own hands by the virtuous and the wise.

I am, very respectfully, dear sir,

Your friend and servant,

JOHN QUINCY ADAMS.

———

TO WILLIAM L. STONE, ESQ.

WASHINGTON, 24 December, 1831.

Dear Sir:—The British acts to parliament, to which I referred in our conversation the other evening, are two,—

1. Statute 37 George 3d, ch. 123, (19th July, 1797,) making the administration of unlawful oaths felony, punishable by transportation for seven years.

2. Statute 39 George 3d, ch. 79, for the suppression of seditious societies (12 July, 1799).

The fifth, sixth, and seventh sections of this last statute except from its penalties, under very rigorous restrictions of police, *the lodges of Freemasons as they have long been usually held in Great Britain;* but not chapters or encampments. From Professor Robinson's book, and other sources, I have been informed that the lodges usually held in Great Britain never confer beyond the first three degrees in Masonry, and content themselves with avenging the murder of Hiram Abiff by those historical personages, Jubela, Jubelo, and Jubelum. I sought you yesterday immediately after the adjournment of the House, in the library of congress, and afterward at Gadsby's without success. It was to give you the above information concerning the British statutes, and to ask the favor of your company to dine with me to-morrow, Christmas day, at five o'clock. Let me expect you, and believe me your assured friend.

JOHN QUINCY ADAMS.

TO WILLIAM L. STONE, ESQ., NEW YORK.

WASHINGTON, 30 June, 1832.

Dear Sir:—I have received your kind letter and the elegant volume which you have done me the honor of addressing to me on the subject of Masonry and Antimasonry. Anticipating in the course of a few days a release from occupations which deprive me at this moment of the power of perusing your work with the deep attention which the importance of the subject requires, I shall avail myself of the first hours at my disposal to devote them to that purpose. In the mean time I cherish the hope that the influence of this comprehensive and impartial survey of the Masonic institutions upon the public mind, will contribute to induce the voluntary abandonment or renunciation of it, which I have long thought, and more firmly believe from day to day, to be desirable for the peace and quiet of the community.

I am, with great respect and esteem, dear sir,

Your friend and obedient servant,

JOHN QUINCY ADAMS.

TO WILLIAM L. STONE, ESQ.

QUINCY, 19 August, 1832.

Dear Sir:—On receiving at Washington the volume of Letters upon Masonry and Antimasonry, which you did me the honor of addressing to me, I wrote you a few lines of acknowledgment, with the assurance of my intention to read with deep attention the work, to the composition and publication of which I felt great satisfaction in believing that I had contributed to give occasion. I have accordingly perused it with the most earnest solicitude, and the result has been not only a confirmed conviction that the institution of Freemasonry ought in these United States to be totally and forever abolished, but that this event is a consummation devoutly to be wished.

In the three letters which I wrote about a year since to a friend in Philadelphia, and which were submitted to your perusal, I presented in the form of interrogation a list of nine atrocious crimes under the denomination of *Morgan - Murder Crimes*, with the inquiry whether they had not been so committed as in a great degree to have lost the character of individual guilt in their perpetrators and to have assumed that of associate or corporate offenses; as conspiracies, in which numerous bodies of men constituting lodges, chapters, and encampments of Freemasons were implicated; and inquiring further, whether the commission of those crimes had not been previously instigated by the oaths administered, the obligations imposed, and the penalties imprecated or denounced, in the ordinary forms of the admission of candidates to the numerously graduated hierarchy of Freemasonry.

That these crimes had been committed,—that the efficient impulse to the commission of them had been the Masonic oaths, obligations, and penalties,—and that they were corporate crimes conceived, projected, and matured for action in the

Masonic deliberative bodies in the western part of the State of New York, I firmly believe from a mass of irresistible evidence, which had been growing into certainty for a series of years. On the other hand, many of the most important facts, both in relation to the commission of the crimes and to the purport of the Masonic oaths and obligations, had been vehemently contested. A considerable number of seceders from Masonry had revealed all the secrets of all the degrees, and all the oaths, and obligations, and penalties, as established in the lodges, chapters, and encampments in all the region round where the murder had been perpetrated. The books of David Bernard and Avery Allyn, both seceding Knights Templars, had been published. Bernard had been admitted to the ineffable degrees in New York, Allyn at New Haven in Connecticut. The Rev. Moses Thatcher and Pliny Merrick had declared that the Royal Arch oath was in many lodges in Rhode Island and Massachusetts administered with the words, "murder and treason not excepted." That it was so administered in the State of New York, had been testimony extorted and most reluctantly given upon oath by Royal Arch Masons upon trials before courts of justice,—and yet adhering Masons were solemnly declaring that *they* had taken no such oaths; that *they*

acknowledged no obligation incompatible with
the laws of God or of the land; that the only
penalty ever inflicted was expulsion; and that
they did not believe the oaths and obligations were
otherwise understood by Masons everywhere.

In the controversial conditions of the facts upon
the issue which seemed to have been made up
between the adhering and the seceding Masons, I
had preferred stating them to our friend at Philadelphia in the form of interrogation rather than
to assume them as granted. He was a Mason,
inclining to Antimasonry, but unwilling to join
its political standard. He knew little of what
had taken place in the western counties of the
State of New York, and had been made to dis-
believe the most prominent facts of the tale of
horror connected with the fate of Morgan. I was
desirous, if possible, to keep myself entirely dis-
entangled from all the politics of Antimasonry;
but this was becoming exceedingly difficult. 'I
wished for a more perfect exposition of facts from
a source fully informed,—from a person in whose
candor and integrity I could place entire reliance,
and not so connected with either of the parties as
to be under a bias disqualifying to the perception
or to the judiciary faculty. I was well assured
that I should find this in your book, and I have
not been disappointed. The book is marked with

integrity and candor, which not even the fifth libation has been able to prevent.

There is a lingering attachment to the institution, as it had been in better days,—like the affection of a parent discovering in bitterness of soul the profligacy of a favorite child,—which adds a double seal of confirmation to the disclosures which you have had the intrepidity to make and to sustain. There are many things in the volume which I do not see as you do; but the sincerity of your own conviction of the truth of all that you affirm is apparent in every page. I speak of the intrepidity of your disclosures, because I have not dissembled to myself the peculiar position in which you stand toward the institution, both as a man and as a member of a responsible profession. I see you as neither an adhering nor a seceding Mason. I think I perceive the conflict in your own mind between the obligation of Masonry which you had taken upon you and the duties of your profession as the editor of a public journal— duties to a community at large, which you had resolved never to compromise or to betray. I think I see that when you took the oaths of the Entered Apprentice, the Master Mason, the Royal Arch, and the Knights Templars, you little imagined the temptations, the trials, and the dangers into which they were to lead you by their conflict

with your duties as a man, a Christian, and a citi‑
zen. You seem scarcely to be aware even now
that the trials through which you are passing
originated there. You are unwilling to acknowl‑
edge it to yourself. But the trials are around
you. You have betrayed no Masonic secret. You
have forfeited no obligations of your own. But
you have justly concluded that of what had been
divulged by others it would be absurd to make
longer a secret, and dishonest to deny it as false.
Yet you are in the midst of brother Masons,—
men whom you respect and esteem, who still
hold themselves bound by the ties which you con‑
sider as dissolved, who still tyle the lodge and
swear the candidates, upon horrible penalties, to
keep secrets now as common as the stairs that
mount the capitol. These men look upon you as
an unworthy brother, even if they have not dared
to expel you. How will these men tolerate your
exposure of the contrast between the public proc‑
lamation and the secret appropriation of the
Grand Royal Arch Chapter of the State of New
York, at which upward of *one hundred and ten
subordinate chapters were represented* in February,
1829, as detailed in your twenty-first letter? How
will they endure your confirmation of the essen‑
tial facts in Avery Allyn's affidavit, that Richard
Howard had confessed himself the executioner of

Morgan; that he made this confession at an encampment of Knights Templars at St. John's Hall, in the city of New York, under the sealed obligation, and had then been furnished with money and means to abscond and go to Europe, as related in your twenty-second letter? How will they bear the twenty-fifth letter? the account of the unblushing grant of money by the grand lodge of the State of New York to one of the most active conspirators? of the debates in which you bore a part? and of the appropriation, since which you have never crossed the threshold of a lodge-room? You are still surrounded by members of the grand lodge, of the grand chapter, and of the encampment at St. John's Hall. And although perhaps you may receive no more letters from Washington like that of the 25th of February, 1827, there are other modes of hostility in which we well know that the Masonic power can make itself felt.

But if the boldness with which you have dared to speak is not without its perils now, neither will it, I trust, be without its remembrance or its recompense hereafter. I believe your letters to be well adapted to promote a great national reform of morals in the abolition of Freemasonry; and the more extensively they are read the more beneficial will be their effect.

This letter is confidential, and if satisfactory to you may be followed by others suggested by the information contained in your book, and perhaps discussing some of your opinions. The Masonic controversy will form a large chapter in the annals of this Union probably for several years to come. It presents already a prominent feature in the canvass for the presidential election, and that is precisely the reason for wishing to meddle as little with it as possible until that question shall have been settled. It will assuredly survive that event, and in all probability will form an essential ingredient in more than one quadrennial choice of president, if more than one we are destined to have. It is my deliberate opinion that the Antimasonic party ought not to subside, or to suspend its exertions, till Freemasonry shall have ceased to exist in this country. The career before them is long and dreary, but not discouraging; the object is single, just, and honorable. You have put your hand to the plow. Let it not be withdrawn. For contributing so largely to the end you will deserve to be ranked among the benefactors of mankind.

I am, very respectfully, your friend,
JOHN QUINCY ADAMS.

TO WILLIAM L. STONE, ESQ.

QUINCY, 25 August, 1832.

Dear Sir:—In my last letter I observed, with the freedom and candor which I thought due to you as the best return I could make for the honor and obligation you had conferred upon me by addressing to me your letters upon Masonry and Antimasonry, that there were many things in the book which I did not see as you did.

Some further explanation is due from me upon the subject. The principal objects of your book were two. First, to vindicate the character of an eminent and illustrious citizen of New York, the late governor of the state, De Witt Clinton, from the opprobrium cast upon him, of having been personally and deeply concerned in the murder of Morgan; and, secondly, to prove, by a fair and impartial statement of the *abuses* to which the Masonic institutions have been perverted, that they ought to be voluntarily surrendered and abolished.

These objects were just and laudable. They are in your volume faithfully perused; nor is there in the execution of your plan anything in the letters unsuited or redundant. You observe,

in the first letter, that it is no part of your design
to write a vindication of Freemasonry as such,
but to describe Freemasonry as you received,
understood, and practiced it yourself, and as it
has been received, understood, and practiced by
hundreds of virtuous and intelligent men, with
whom you have associated in the lodge-room. To
this, the first ten letters are devoted, and they are
in my estimation not less valuable than those
which succeed them.   But as Bishop Watson
wrote an apology for the Bible, I trust you will
not consider me as intending any disparagement
to that part of your work, if I consider it in the
light of an apology for Freemasonry, as received,
understood, and practiced by yourself and many
others.   In that light it is exceedingly well
adapted to its purpose. It is the only rational
plea for the institution that I have seen since this
controversy began, for all the other defenses of
the handmaid, which have come to my knowledge, have smacked too much of the obligation
to come to the aid of a distressed brother and
extricate him from his difficulties *right or wrong*,
to pass for anything other than aggravations of
the Morgan-murder crimes.

You have taken all the degrees to, and
including that of, the Knight Templar. The
oaths, obligations, and penalties, as administered

to and understood by you, contained nothing
incompatible with your duties to your country
and your kind. Whatever there might be in
them, apparently incongruous with the prior and
paramount duties of the citizen and Christian,
was explained and given in charge in such manner as to be made entirely subordinate to them.
The obligations, as understood by you, are all
auxiliaries to Christian benevolence and patriot-
ism, and so they are undoubtedly understood by
great multitudes of Masons in all parts of the
United States. That they are otherwise understood, also, by multitudes of the *worthy* brethren
of the craft (worthy according to the *Masonic*
meaning of the word) is apparent in every page
of your book.

In your third letter, page 23, you allude to an
opinion which I once expressed to you in the following terms: " You, sir, have assured me that
the obligations supposed to be administered in
conferring the first degree is quite enough in your
view to establish the wicked character of the
institution."

Whether I did make use of terms quite so
strong in the freedom of unrestrained conversation, or whether your reference to it is by
inference of your own, from words not quite so
comprehensive, is not material. The sentiment

which I do recollect to have expressed, and which is rooted in my conviction, was, "that the Entered Apprentice's oath, obligation, and annexed penalty, was in itself *vicious*, and such as ought never to be administered by man to man;" that no explanation of it could take away its essentially immoral character, and that the institution of Freemasonry, requiring absolutely the administration of it to every candidate for admission, necessarily shared in its immorality.

In saying this, I disclaim all intention of censure upon any individual who has ever taken this oath. I consider it according to its own import—stripped of all warrant of authority from the great names of illustrious men who may have taken it.

My objections to it are these:

1. That it is an extrajudicial oath, and, as such, contrary to the laws of the land.

2. That it is a violation of the precept of Jesus Christ—*swear not at all.*

3. That this oath pledges the candidate, in the name of God, that he will always hail, forever conceal, and never reveal any of the *secret arts, parts, or points of the mysteries* " *of Freemasonry,* to any person under the canopy of heaven, except it shall be to a true and lawful Mason, or within the body of a just and regular lodge of such, and not

unto him or them until after due trial, strict examination, or by the lawful information of a brother, I shall have found him or them as justly and lawfully entitled to the same as I am myself."

The arts, parts, points, and mysteries of Masonry are afterward, in the oath. denominated the *secrets of the craft.* These are general and indefinite terms. The candidate, when he takes the oath, is kept in total ignorance of what these *secrets of the craft* consist. *He knows not the nature nor extent of the oath that he takes.* He is sworn to keep secret he *knows not what.* The general assurance that it is not to affect his religion or politics is the mere word of another man. The assurance that it is not to interfere with any of his duties is but a mockery, when the administration of the oath itself is a violation of law.

He swears to reveal the secrets of the craft to no person under the canopy of heaven, *except* to a brother Mason, or a lodge. The single exception expressed is an exclusion of all others. There is no exception for the authority of law, or for the confession enjoined upon the Catholic brethren by their religion. I use this illustration to show that the intrinsic import of the oath is incompatible with law, civil and religious.

Now what these secrets of the craft are to the keeping of which the candidate, thus ignorant of

their import, is sworn, is never defined. They
are differently understood by different Masons.
The oaths, obligations, and penalties themselves
have, until very recently, been understood, I
believe, universally to form a part of these secrets.
Those of the first three degrees were first revealed
by the publication of Morgan's book; those of
the subsequent degrees, to that of the thrice illustrious order of the cross, were divulged by the
convention of the seceding Masons at Le Roy, on
the 4th of July, 1828. Those in Morgan's book I
understand to be admitted on all hands to be correct. But with regard to the obligation of the
Red Cross Knights and the Templars, as disclosed
by that convention, you say that, although you
have received those degrees and assisted in conferring them, you know of no such obligations in
any of the degrees. Your impression is that they
must have been devised westward of Albany and
imposed upon candidates without the sanction of
any governing body. You do not question the
correctness of the publication of these degrees by
the convention of seceding Masons. You are
authorized to state that when the forms of those
obligations were received in the city, measures
were taken by the grand encampment to ascer-
tain whether any encampment under its jurisdiction had, in fact, ever administered any such

obligations, and if so, where and by whom they had been imposed.

It is earnestly to be hoped that the grand encampment will sincerely and seriously pursue this inquiry, and make known the result of their researches to the world. In the mean time, observe the inferences to be drawn from this extreme diversity of the terms and import of the obligations as administered in different lodges, chapters, and encampments; but *all* under the sanction of this tremendous oath of the Entered pledge, given in advance, and in ignorance of Apprentice; all secured by this soul-shackling what they are to be, and all riveted by the penalty to which I shall next advert.

4. " All this I promise and swear, binding myself under no less penalty than that of having my throat cut across from ear to ear, my tongue torn out by its roots, and my body buried in the rough sand of the sea, at low-water mark, where the tide ebbs and flows twice in twenty-four hours."

We have been told, over and over again, that this is understood by Masons to be merely an invocation; and the committee of investigation of the legislature of Rhode Island have gravely told the world that the explanation given by Masons to this *penalty* is, " that I would rather have,

or sooner have, my throat cut than to reveal," &c.
It is unfortunate that this explanation is in direct
contradiction to the plain and unequivocal import
of the words of the oath. The oath incurs the
penalty for its violation. The explanation promises
fidelity, though at the expense of life. The oath
imprecates the death of a traitor, as a *penalty* for
treachery. The explanation claims a crown of
martyrdom for constancy. If Benedict Arnold
had been taken in the act of treason to his
country, he would have suffered no less a *penalty*
than death—though not the barbarous and brutal
death of the Masonic obligation. When Joseph
Warren suffered death on Bunker Hill, is there
an explanatory Mason who dare tell you that he
suffered a *penalty?* Yet so it is that the Masonic
oath, and its explanation, confound all moral distinctions to the degree of considering the death
of a martyr and the death of a traitor as one and
the same thing.

This *explanation* of the penalty annexed to the
Entered Apprentice's oath, it must be acknowl-
edged, is not ingenuous,—it is not even ingenious.
It is a grand hailing sign of distress; or it is a
Masonic murder of the English language.

I say this with the less hesitation, because in
your seventh letter, containing *your* defense of the
Masonic obligations, you have disdained to take

this preposterous *explanation* of the Rhode Island Masons. You know too well the import of words. You candidly avow that the oaths and obligations are out of season,—out of reason,—and ought to be abolished. I will therefore forbear to press upon you the still grosser absurdity of the pretended Rhode Island explanation, when applied to the Master Mason's and Royal Arch penalties. The Master Mason's penalty is to have his body severed in two in the midst, and divided to the north and south, his bowels burnt to ashes in the center, and the ashes scattered before the four winds of heaven, *that there might not the least track or trace of remembrance remain among men or Masons of so vile and perjured a wretch as I should be.* And this, according to the Rhode Island explanation, is to be the consequence of his dying like Hiram Abiff, rather than betray the Masonic secrets.

My fifth objection is to the horrible *ideas* of which the penalty is composed. It is an oath of which a common cannibal should be ashamed. Even in the barbarous ages of antiquity, Homer tells you that when Achilles dragged the dead body of Hector round the walls of Troy, it was a dishonest deed,— *aeikea medeto erga;* and Plato severely censures Homer for even introducing this incident into his poem. A mangled body, after death, was a thought disgusting even to heathens. From the very thoughts, and still more from the lips, of a Christian it should be forever excluded, like indelicacy from the mouth of a female. The constitution of the United States, and of Massachusetts, prohibit the infliction of cruel or unusual punishments, even by the authority of the law. But no butcher would mutilate the carcass of a bullock or swine, as the Masonic candidate swears consent to the mutilation of his own, for the breach of an absurd and senseless secret. I can not assent to your denomination of these penalties as idle or unmeaning words. They are words of too much meaning—of hideous significancy. The Masons are bound for their own honor to expunge them from their records forever. Would that they could be expunged from the language, dishonored by their introduction into its forms of speech.

I remain, very respectfully, your friend,
JOHN QUINCY ADAMS.

TO WILLIAM L. STONE, ESQ.

QUINCY, 29 August, 1832.

Dear Sir:—Long, and, I fear, tedious, as you have found my last letter, I was compelled by a reluctance at making it longer, to compress the observations in it upon the *intrinsic* nature of the Masonic *oaths, obligations,* and *penalties* within a compass insufficient to disclose my opinion, and the reasons upon which it is founded.

I had said to you that the institution of Freemasonry was *vicious,* in its first step, the initiation *oath, obligation,* and *penalty* of the Entered Apprentice. To sustain this opinion, I assigned to you five reasons. Because they were,

1. Contrary to the laws of the land, extrajudicially taken and administered.

2. In violation of the *positive* precept of Jesus Christ.

3. A pledge to keep *undefined* secrets, the swearer being ignorant of their nature.

4. A pledge to the penalty of death *for* violation of the oath.

5. A pledge to a *mode* of death—cruel, unusual, unfit for utterance from human lips.

If, in the statement of these five *objections,* upon

principles of law, religion, and morals, there be anything unsound, I invite you to point it out. But if you contest either of my positions, I must entreat you not to *travel out of the record.*

I might ask you not to consider it a refutation of either of these reasons, to say that you and all other honest and honorable Masons have never so understood or practiced upon this oath, obligation, and penalty. The inquiry is not what you practice, or that of others has been, but what *is* the obligation, its oath, and its penalty.

I must request of you to give me no *explanation* of this oath, obligation, and penalty, directly contrary to their unequivocal import,—that you will not explain *black* by saying that it means *white,* or even by alleging that you so understand it. I particularly beg not to be told that honorable, intelligent, and virtuous men—George Washington and Joseph Warren for example—understood that the penalty of death for treachery meant the death of martyrdom for fidelity.

I would willingly be spared the necessity of replying to the averment that the patterns of honor and virtue whom I have just named, with a long catalogue of such men, *have* taken this oath, and bound themselves to this obligation, under this penalty; for I might deem it proper to inquire whether the very act of binding such men, by such oath, to such obligation, under such penalty, is not among the *sins* of the institution.

I must ask you to suppose that such institution had never existed,— that it were now to be formed, and that you were one of ten or twenty virtuous and intelligent men about to found a charitable and convivial secret association. Suppose a committee of such a meeting appointed to draw up a constitution for the society should report the Entered Apprentice's oath, obligation, and penalty, as a form of initiation for the admission of members. I do not ask you whether you would vote for the acceptance of the report; but what would you think of the reporters?

I consider this as the true and only test of the inherent and essential character of Masonry, and it was under this conviction that I told you that the Entered Apprentice's oath was sufficient to settle, in my mind, the immoral character of the institution.

It is, perhaps, too much to ask of you an explicit assent to these positions, because you may consider it an acknowledgment of error. But this is the first and fundamental consideration, from which I draw the conclusion that Masonry *ought* forever to be abolished. It is wrong,— essentially wrong,—a seed of evil which can never produce any good. It may perish in the ground — it may never rise to bear fruit; but whatever fruit it does bear must be rank poison ; it can never prove a blessing but by its barrenness.

My objections to this *seminal principle* of Masonry apply, in all their force, to the single obligation, the form of which is given in the appendix to your volume (page 3), where it is stated to have been the only obligation, taken for all three degrees, so late as 1730, when only three degrees of Masonry were known. The oath is in fewer words, but more comprehensive; for the obligation is to keep " *the secrets or secrecy of Masons or Masonry.*" There is indeed a qualification in the promise not to write, print, mark, &c., which seems to keep the obligations within the verge of the law. For the promise is to reveal nothing whereby the secret might be *unlawfully* obtained. The penalty is also death, not for constancy, but for treachery, " so that there shall be no remembrance of me among Masons."

The oath, obligation, and penalty, the only one taken in all the degrees of Masonry known but one century ago, is the prolific parent of all the degrees, and all the oaths, obligations, and penalties since invented, and of the whole progeny of crimes descended from them. The natural and unavoidable tendency of such an obligation is the multiplication of its kind. This tendency is

among the most obvious causes which have led to
the interdiction of *all* such oaths and obligations,
by the civil, the ecclesiastical, and the moral law.
The obligation is to keep *undefined* secrets. As
they are undefined in the obligation itself, there
is nothing in the constitutions of Masonry to
define them, or to secure uniformity either of the
secrets or of the obligations. Every lodge may
vary the secrets, obligations, and penalties; and,
accordingly, they have been so varied that
scarcely any two adhering Masons give the same
account of them. Almost the only defense of .
Masonry, after the publication of the books of
David Bernard and Avery Allyn, consisted in
efforts to discredit them, by denying that the
oaths, obligations, and penalties were truly stated
by them. A secret institution in three degrees,
the secret of each degree being withheld from
the members of the degrees inferior to it, is a
perpetual temptation to the initiated to multiply
the secrets and the degrees. Thus it is that the
lodges have grown into chapters, the chapters
into encampments, the encampments into con-
sistories; and, so long ago as December, 1802, the
grand inspectors of the United States of America
issued, at Charleston, South Carolina, a circular
announcing the existence and names of the thirty-
three degrees of Masonry.

8

The secrets, to the keeping of which the Entered Apprentice is sworn, are *indefinite*. In genuine Masonry, when revealed to him, he finds them *frivolous*. You acknowledged that your first feeling upon receiving them was disappointment. So must it be with every reflecting, intelligent man; nor is it conceivable that any such Entered Apprentice, on leaving the lodge after his admission, should fail to have observed, with pain and mortification, the contrast between the awful solemnity of the oath which he has taken, and the extreme insignificance of the secrets revealed to him. It is to meet this unavoidable impression that the institution is graduated. The lure of curiosity is still held out, and its attractive power is sinewed, by the very disappointment which the apprentice has experienced. He takes the degrees of Fellowcraft and Master Mason, and still finds disappointment — still finds himself bound by tremendous oaths to keep trifling and frivolous secrets. The practice of the institution is deceptive and fraudulent. It holds out to him a promise which it never performs. Its promise is light; its performance is darkness.

But it introduces him to intimate, confidential, and exclusive relations, with a select and limited circle of other men,—and to the same confidential and exclusive relations, with great multitudes of men belonging to every civilized nation throughout the globe. The Entered Apprentice's oath is merely an oath of secrecy; but the candidate who takes it has pledged himself, by his application for admission, to conform to all the ancient established usages and customs of the fraternity. And the charge of the master, given him upon the Bible, compasses, and square, presents him with three precious jewels,—a *listening ear*, a *silent tongue*, and a *faithful heart*,—all, of course, exclusively applicable to the *secrets* revealed to him; and he is told that the listening ear teaches him to listen to the instructions of the worshipful master, but more especially to the cries of a worthy distressed brother; and the faithful heart teaches him to be faithful to the instructions of the worshipful master at all times, but more especially to keep and conceal the secrets of Masonry, *and those of a brother*, when given to him in charge as such, that they may remain as secure and inviolable in his (the Entered Apprentice's) breast as in his (the brother's) own. Two check-words are also presented to him,—*truth* and *union*, —the explanation of which concludes that the heart and tongue of Freemasons join in promoting *each other's* welfare, and rejoicing in each other's prosperity.

Thus the essential nature of the Entered Apprentice's oath, preceded by his pledge to conform to all the established usages and customs of the fraternity, and followed by the charge of the master, is *secret* and *exclusive* favor, assistance, and fidelity *to the brotherhood and brothers of the craft.*

Now combine together the disappointment which every intelligent accepted Mason must feel, at the puerility of the secrets revealed to him, compared with the appalling solemnity of the oath exacted from him for the purchase of his lambskin apron, and the secret ties with which he has linked himself with multitudes of other men, exclusively to favor, assist, and be faithful to each other, and acknowledge that the temptation to make the secrets more important, and to turn them to better account to the craft, must be irresistible. Judge this system *a priori*, without reference to any of the consequences which it has produced, and say if human ingenuity could invent an engine better suited to conspiracy of any kind. The Entered Apprentice returns from the lodge with his curiosity stimulated, his imagination bewildered, and his reason disappointed. The mixture of religion and morality, blended with falsehood and imposture, which pervade all the ceremonies of initiation, is like arsenic mingled up with balm.

"Most dangerous
Is that temptation which doth lead us on
To sin in loving virtue."

If the candidate has been educated to a sincere
and heart-felt reverence for religion and the Bible,
and if he exercises his reason he *knows* that all
the tales of Jachin and Boaz, of Solomon's temple, of Hiram Abiff and Jubela, Jubelo, and
Jubelum, are impostures,—poisons poured into
the perennial fountain of truth,—traditions ex-
actly resembling those reprobated by Jesus Christ,
as making the word of God of none effect. If,
as in this age but too often happens, he enters the
lodge a skeptic, the use of the Bible there, if it
have any effect upon him, will turn him out a
confirmed infidel. The sincere and rational be-
liever in the gospel can find no confirmation of
his faith in the unwarrantable uses made of the
Holy Scriptures to shed an unction of their
sanctity around the fabulous fabric of Freemasonry; while the reprobate miscreant will be
taught the uses to which fraud and secrecy may
turn the lessons of piety and virtue, inculcated in
the sublimest effusions of divine inspiration. In
those Scriptures we are told that when "the children of Israel did *secretly* those things that were
not right against the Lord their God," they
became idolators, and were carried into captivity.

Their cities then were soon filled with a mongrel race of Babylonians and Assyrians, who perverted the word of God with the impostures of paganism; burned their children in fire, to the gods of Sepharvaim; and "*feared* the Lord and *served* their graven images,"—an emblem of Freemasonry far more illustrative of its character than the tragedy of Hiram Abiff.

The Entered Apprentice's oath is, therefore, in its own nature, a seminal principle of conspiracy; and this objection applies to the only oath originally taken in all the degrees of Freemasonry at its first institution. The *ostensible* primitive purposes of Freemasonry were all comprised in *good fellowship*. But to good fellowship, whether of labor or refreshment, neither secrecy, nor oath, nor penalties are necessary or congenial. In the original institution of Freemasonry there was then an ostensible and a secret object, and by the graduation of the order the means were supplied of converting it to any *evil* purpose of associated power, screened from the danger of detection. Hence, all the bitter fruits which the institution has borne in Germany, in France, in Mexico, and lastly, in this our beloved country. Nor could they have failed to be produced in Great Britain, but that, by sharp and biting statutes, they have been confined within the limits of the ostensible object of the brotherhood—good fellowship.

am, with much respect, dear sir,

Your friend and servant,

JOHN QUINCY ADAMS.

TO WILLIAM L. STONE, ESQ.

QUINCY, 6 September, 1832.

Dear Sir:—In my two preceding letters you have seen my objections drawn from the fountains of law, religion, and morals, against the first step of Freemasonry,—the *oath*, with its obligation and penalty, administered to the Entered Apprentice at his initiation. You will certainly understand that, in this denunciation of the *thing*, it is not my intention to include a charge against any individual who has ever taken the oath; as, on the other hand, I exclude all palliation or justification of it, upon the mere authority of the great names of men by whom it has been taken.

It is a pledge of faith from man to man solemnized by an appeal to God, and fortified by the express assent of the swearer to undergo the penalty of death, and mutilation at or after death, for its violation. Such it is in itself, and no explanation can, without doing violence to the natural connection between thought and language, take away this its essential and unequivocal import.

The objections are, 1. To the oath. 2. To the promise. 3. To the penalty.

1. *To the oath*, as a double violation of the law of the land, and of the law of God. Upon this there appears, by your seventh letter, to be very little if any difference of opinion between you and me. The principles assumed and admitted in the introduction to your seventh letter are unquestionably correct with reference to law, to religion, and to morals; and it is equally clear that they are all disregarded in the administration of the Masonic oaths. It is a vice of the institution which no example can justify, and which no sophistry can extenuate. Your acknowledgement is magnanimous—your argument unanswerable.

But if the administration of the oath is, of itself, a violation of the laws both of God and man, as well by him who administers as by him who takes it, is it not a further mockery of both, for the master, in the very act of transgressing the laws, and of suborning the candidate to transgress them with him, to say to him, "This obligation is not intended to interfere with your duty to yourself, your neighbor, your country, or your God." Is there not falsehood and hypocrisy superadded to the breach of the law, and profanation of the name of God, in the injunction and explanation itself? He calls upon the candidate to perform an unlawful act; and he tells him that it is not to interfere with his religion or politics, or, with deeper duplicity, that it is to interfere with none of his civil, moral, or religious duties. This self-contradiction of word and deed is the very essence of all sanguinary religious fanaticism. It is the very vital spark of the spirit which armed with daggers the hands of Ravaillac Balthasar Girard. Under the excruciating pangs of the torture, Ravaillac, to his last gasp, protested that he thought he was serving God by the assassination of a king who was about to declare war against the pope; and he signed his name to one of the interrogatories at his trial — François Ravaillac—

> Qeu toujours dans mon cœur
> Jesus soit le vainqueur.

> " In my heart, forever, may
> Jesus hold conquering sway."

If the murder of Henry IV., of France, had been concerted in a Masonic lodge-room, and the master had administered to the perpetrator, as a part of his oath, the obligation to commit that deed, he might, with just as much reason and consistency, have assured him that this oath would not interfere with his religion or politics, or with his duty to himself, his neighbor, his country, or his God, as the master of a Masonic lodge can now give such an assurance to a candidate for admission before administering to him the oath of an Entered Apprentice.

2. *To the promise.*

The promise is to keep the secrets of Masonry, and never to reveal them to any human being not already initiated. I have already objected that this promise is indefinite. The promiser knows not the nature of the secrets he is sworn to keep; nor are they ever explained to him. In your seventh letter (page 71) you have explicitly stated your own understanding of what the secrets were, and that you have always found your *intelligent* brethren ready to concur in that opinion. Your definition of them is so clear and satisfactory that, if it were in its very terms so explained by the master, before administering the oath, *this* objection would be removed.

" The essential secrets of Masonry (you say) consisted in nothing more than the signs, grips, pass-words, and tokens, essential to the preservation of the society from the inroads of impostors, together with certain symbolical emblems, the technical terms appertaining to which served as a sort of universal language, by which the members of the fraternity could distinguish each other, in all places and countries where lodges were instituted and conducted like those of the United States."

In *nothing more.* But no such explanation is ever given to the candidate for admission, when the oath is administered to him, or ever afterward; and you candidly admit that this is not the understanding entertained of the secrets of Masonry, by "the foolish brethren." Now, herein consists my objection to the promise. It is to keep secret he knows not what, — he never knows, — and this indefiniteness is essential to preserve the graduation of the order. It is essential to keep alive the *curiosity* of the candidate who, at each degree that he attains, is always comforted in his disappointment by the assurance that there is, in the next degree, a secret worth knowing.

If it be said that the exaction of a promise to keep a secret must necessarily precede the communication of the secret itself, and that, therefore, no promiser can know in advance what it is that he pledges himself to keep secret, I reply that my objection is to the indefiniteness not only of the secret itself, but of the promise. Jurors in courts of law are sworn to keep secret the counsels of their fellows and their own. The juror, to be sure, knows not what the counsels of his fellows will be, when he swears to keep them secret, but he knows that they can not extend beyond the line of their duty to decide the matter committed to them,—and there is nothing indefinite in the obligation from the moment when it becomes binding upon him. The Masonic swearer is ignorant of the extent both of the oath and of his promise,—and after his admission he still is never informed what are the secrets which he has been sworn to keep.

In *your* enumeration of the essential secrets of the order, you do not include the oaths themselves, as administered to the candidates for admission. These, therefore, are not secrets which any Mason is bound to keep. But has this been the understanding of *intelligent* Masons heretofore? Why, then, have the forms of the oaths never been made public in the Masonic books published by authority, or without objection from the order? Why have they become so different in different places? Why, in all the trials which have arisen from the murder of Morgan, and in which evidence of the forms of these oaths, obligations, and penalties was essential to the issue, have not authenticated copies of them been produced in court by the Masonic witnesses themselves? In Massachusetts, in Vermont, in Rhode Island, there have been numerous *defenses* of Masonry, by individual Masons and Masonic lodges, very indignantly denying that *they* ever took or administered the obligation with the words, "murder and treason not excepted;" and generally denying that they were under any obligation contrary to the laws of God, or that of their country. But anxious as they have all been to fix the charge of *slander* upon Avery Allyn and David Bernard, and to make the world believe that the forms of Masonic oaths, obligations, and penalties, disclosed in their books, were fabrications of their own, never used by any Masonic body, still, in no single instance have they ever produced or certified to the oaths, obligations, and penalties as used or administered by themselves, until the investigation instituted last winter by the legislature of Rhode Island, and conducted in a spirit so friendly to Masonry, and so adverse to Antimasonry,.that it could scarcely have been more so, had every member of the investigating committee but one been himself an adhering Mason. In that investigation the committee, like yourself, considered the secrets of Masonry to consist of the signs, grips, pass-words, and emblematic figures of speech, and no more,—

and, with regard to these, they indulged the brotherhood, not by inquiring into them, by interrogation of adhering Masons,—giving notice that they should take all these profound mysteries to have been correctly set forth in the books of Allyn and Bernard, unless positive testimony to the contrary should be voluntarily offered by adhering Masons.

But the committee did require testimony from the adhering Masons, of the oaths, obligations, and penalties, as taken in the lodges, chapters, and encampments in Rhode Island, and it was given. The appendix to the report of the committee contains this evidence, and authenticates upon full, adhering Masonic authority, the oaths, obligations, and penalties, as taken and administered in Rhode Island, of eleven degrees, from the Entered Apprentice to the Royal Master.

It is, therefore, to the *indefiniteness* of the promise in this authenticated obligation of the Entered Apprentice that I take my first objection,—and this indefiniteness is not only intrinsic in the terms of the obligation itself, but is aggravated by the previous pledge of the candidate to conform to the established usages and customs of the order, and by the charge given by the master who administers the oath, which charge enjoins it upon the candidate as a duty to obey the instructions of the master of the lodge, and to keep the secrets of a brother Mason, committed to him as such. The obligation includes also the pledge to keep secret the transactions of the lodge —without exception.

There are thus, according to the understanding of the Rhode Island Masons, and to yours, *three* distinct classes of secrets to which every accepted Mason was bound. First, to the secrets of Masonry, consisting only of the signals of communition and tokens of mutual recognition between the members of the fraternity; secondly, the secrets of brother Masons, communicated as such; and, thirdly, the transactions in the lodge. And of these, you and they consider the first class only as essential to the order. But what is the principle of this distinction? None such is found in the oaths themselves, nor in any of the Masonic books, nor in the charges given by the master to the candidate for admission. Does the promise of secrecy, given by the Entered Apprentice, extend to the *transactions of the lodge?* It does not, in the terms of the oath. It does not, by the practice of the Rhode Island lodges,—for they enjoin this portion of the secrets by their by-laws upon the penalty of *expulsion;* but those same by-laws contain no provision whatever for the violation of the *essential* secrets. In all the oaths

and obligations *subsequent* to the degree of the
Entered Apprentice, the promise includes the
secrets of a brother Mason, communicated as
such, but not the transactions of the lodge, chapter, or encampment.   These are deemed binding
only by virtue of the other promise of the candidate, that he will conform to the usages, customs,
and regulations of the fraternity.   But this distinction itself proves that, in Masonic contemplation, the obligation to keep secret the transactions
of the lodge is not the obligation, with the oath
and penalty, to keep the essential secrets of the
craft.   For disclosing the transactions of the
lodge, the penalty is expulsion.   But the by-laws
contain no such penalty for disclosing the secrets
of the craft.   What is this but a recognition that
the penalty for divulging the secrets of the craft
is different from the penalty for revealing the
transactions of the lodge?—that it is a crime of
much higher order, sanctioned by the oath with
its penalty, and for which it would be alike inconsistent and absurd to provide by a by-law or reg-
ulation of the lodge.

My first objection to the *promise* of the Entered
Apprentice's obligation is its *indefiniteness*,—and
this objection extends to all the obligations of the
subsequent degrees, and to the institution itself,
which is nowhere limited to any number of

degrees, and is thereby rendered a ready engine of conspiracy for any evil purpose.

A second objection to the *promise* is its *universality.* It is to keep the secrets of the craft, and never to reveal them to *any person under the canopy of heaven.* The single exception has no other effect than to exclude all other exceptions. It is confined to initiated brothers and regular lodges, to whom the Entered Apprentice can, of course, reveal nothing, they being already in possession of secrets which he promises to keep. The promise, therefore, is never to reveal the secrets of Masonry *to any person under the canopy of heaven.*

I shall pursue this subject in another letter.

JOHN QUINCY ADAMS.

————

TO WILLIAM L. STONE, ESQ.

QUINCY, 10 September, 1832.

Dear Sir.—The second objection to the *promise* of the Entered Apprentice's obligation is its *universality.* The candidate swears that he will never reveal any of the undefined " arts, parts, or points of the mysteries of Freemasonry, *to any person under the canopy of heaven.*" This promise, like the administration of the oath, is, in its terms, contrary to the law of the land. The laws of this, and every civilized country, make it the duty of every citizen to testify the whole truth of facts, deemed by legislative bodies or judicial tribunals, material to the issue of the investigation before them. It is also the duty of a good citizen to denounce and *reveal* to the authorities established to execute the laws against criminals, any secret crimes of which he has in any manner acquired the knowledge. Now, there is nothing in the *arts, parts, or points of the mysteries of Freemasonry* which, in the trial of a judicial cause, or in an investigation of a legislative assembly, may not be justly deemed material to the issue before the court or the legislature. Of its materiality, the judges or the legislators have the exclusive right to decide. No witness, called before the court of justice or an authorized committee of a legislature, can refuse to answer any question put to him by the court or the committee, on the ground that *he* deems it immaterial to the trial before them. This principle becomes more glaringly obvious, when applied to the *promise* never to reveal the secrets of a brother Mason, communicated to him as such, contained in the Master Mason's oath. But the principle is identically the same. The Entered Apprentice promises

never to reveal to any person under the canopy
of heaven, *that* which the laws of his country
may, the next day after he makes the promise,
make it his duty to reveal to any court of justice
before which he may be summoned to appear, or
to any committee of the legislature of the state in
which he resides, or of the Union. The promise
is therefore unlawful, by its universality.

You will remember that I am maintaining the
position that the obligation, under oath and penalty, administered to and taken by the Entered
Apprentice, is, *in itself*, essentially vicious. I now
state the promise in the words universally admitted to be used in that ceremony. Do you deny
that they contain an unlawful promise? Yes,
say you, because the candidate is told, by the
master who administers the oath, that "he is expressly to understand that nothing therein contained is to interfere with his political or religious
principles, with his duty to God, or the laws of
his country." And you, and all honest and
worthy Masons, take and administer the oath
with this understanding. Well, then, the promise
is, in its terms, contrary to the law of the land,—
but you take and administer it with *tacit* reservation, furnished to you not by the action of your
own understanding, but by the previous notifica-
tion of the master who administers the oath to

you. So, and so only, you say, the terms of the promise are to be construed. But, in the first place, this is not a question of construction, but a question of mental reservation. The words are plain and unequivocal; but you pronounce them with a reservation, that the promise shall bind you to nothing contrary to law. Now, what possible reason or justification can there be for exacting a promise, under oath, the real meaning of which is totally different from that of the terms in which it is couched? You swear a man to one thing, and you tell him it means another. But, secondly, how far does your exception extend? You say the promise extends only to the essential secrets of Masonry, and to the lawful transactions in the lodges, and to the secrets of Masons, not criminal,—the former of which you consider of not the least consequence to the world, but essential for the preservation of the society. The secrecy of transactions in the lodges you believed to be merely conventional; and the promise of keeping the secrets of a brother Mason are cancelled, when the secret confided to you by him is of a crime committed by himself.

Now, all these exceptions resolve themselves into the tacit reservation, authorized by the declaration of the master, before administering the oath, that it contains nothing contrary to law.

If the oath is taken with that reservation, it applies equally to the promise to keep the *essential* secrets of the order, and to all the others. And, therefore, a Freemason, summoned before the committee of a legislature or a court of justice, is bound not less to disclose the grips, signs, due guards, and tokens, than he is to divulge the crimes of a brother Mason, known to him.

The simple question I take to be this: I suppose a Freemason to be summoned before a legislative committee or assembly, or judicial tribunal, to testify. Is he or is he not bound to answer any interrogatory put to him by their authority, and which they require of him to answer, respecting *the essential secrets of the craft?* If he is, how can these secrets be kept, and of what avail are all the oaths administered to Masonic candidates, whether with or without penalty? If he is not, then the obligation oath supersedes the obligation of the law of the land. And if the Masonic oath of secrecy is paramount to the law of the land, with regard to the *mysteries of the craft*, where is the principle which *restores* the supremacy of the law, to require the disclosure of the Masonic crimes? The Masonic oath makes no discrimination between the secrets,—the promise to keep them all. The declaration of the master that there is nothing *unlawful* in the oath, makes no discrimination,—it applies to all, or it applies to none.

With this view of the subject, you will perceive that I deem it altogether immaterial to the argument, whether the words " murder and treason not excepted" are or are not included in the Royal Arch Mason's promise of secrecy,—whether he promise to espouse the cause of a brother Mason, right or wrong, or not,—and whether the words, " and they left to my own election," are or are not an innovation in the Master Mason's oath. But when you ask me, as an act of "justice, to believe that, should a brother Mason tell you, as a secret, that he had robbed a store, you would very speedily make the matter public in the police office," I must, while very cheerfully and sincerely believing you, observe that it would be at the expense of the very explicit import of the Master Mason's oath. By that oath the Master Mason promises to keep the secrets of a brother Master Mason as secure and inviolable as if they were in his own breast, " murder and treason excepted." That is, excepting two specific enumerated crimes. What, then, is the meaning of this exception, and why are they excepted? The naming of them emphatically leaves all other crimes included in the *promise* and *excluded* from the exception. The Master Mason's promise does, therefore, by the plain import of its terms, pledge him to keep secret the knowledge of any crime committed by a brother Master Mason, and communicated to him as a Masonic secret, other than the two specified by name; and if you should be in the unfortunate condition of having such a secret communicated to you, and should give notice of it at the police office, you would discharge your duty to your country, only by considering your Masonic promise as null and void. For here is the dilemma. If the Masonic promises are *all* made with the tacit reservation that *nothing* contrary to law is understood to be included in them, then the exception of murder and treason in the Master Mason's oath is not only superfluous, but deceptive,—since it limits to two specific crimes, the exception already referred to, of all crimes whatsoever. And if the Masonic promises are made without the reserved exception of *all* unlawful things, then the exception of murder and treason, from the secrets which the Master Mason pledges himself to keep, leaves all other crimes as distinctly under the shelter of the promise as if they had been included in it expressly by name

3. *To the promise.* Death by torture and mutilation.

I have, in a former letter, exposed the fallacy—

I must say the disgenuous fallacy — of the attempt to defend this part of the Masonic obligation in the late Rhode Island legislative inves-. tigation. In the tale of "January and May," when the doting, blind, and abused husband, by the miraculous interposition of the king of the fairies, receives instantaneous restoration of sight to witness his own dishonor, the queen of fairies, with equal promptitude, suggests to the guilty wife an *explanation*. The Masonic brotherhood of Rhode Island are as ready to take a suggestion from the queen of fairies as the youthful and *studious* May. The committee of the Rhode Island legislature was composed of men too intelligent to be duped like the wittol January; yet were they contented to be told, and to believe, that the penalty of death *for* revealing a secret, was identically one and the same thing as the heroic martyrdom of death *rather* than to reveal a secret. All language is a system of logic; all language is a system of morals; all figurative language is translation. The words may say one thing and intend another; but translation must not confound moral distinctions, and irony and denuncications are the only figures of speech which are permitted in human intercourse to "wash an Ethiop white.'

Your own exposition of this penalty is more

candid and more plausible. You consider the words in which the penalty is expressed as *unmeaning*, because the candidate has been told that the obligation contains nothing contrary to law; and because the society neither possesses nor exercises the power to authorize the execution of the penalty. This, of course, considers the penalty as null and void.

And so, one would think, it *must* be considered by every fair-minded and honorable man. And why, then, do fair-minded and honorable men adhere to this penalty? Is it worthy for fair-minded and honorable men to use words full of sound and fury, signifying nothing? to use them as the sanction of a promise? to use them with an appeal to the everlasting God? Are the words so charming in themselves, is the thought conveyed by them to the mind so irresistibly fascinating, that even now twelve hundred fair-minded and honorable men of Massachusetts declare, in the face of their country and of mankind, that they will not renounce the use of them? Oh, say not what fair-minded and honorable men will or will not do! Twelve hundred men of Massachusetts, men of fair and honorable minds, even now, after all the arts, parts, and points of the mysteries of Freemasonry have been revealed and published to the world, nay, after the very check-word, transmitted to them for their protection against the intrusion of book-Masons upon their mysteries, had been divulged with all the rest,—after all this, twelve hundred Masons of Massachusetts have declared that they will not renounce or abandon the mysteries of Freemasonry; that they will still continue to hold their meetings, to tyle their lodges, to brandish their drawn swords for the exclusion of cowans and eavesdroppers, and to swear the knave or simpleton who will henceforth submit to take the oath, never to reveal, never to write, print, cut, carve, paint, stain, or engrave, secrets known to every one who will take the trouble to read,—secrets, in their own estimation, insignificant and puerile,—secrets, in the estimation of great multitudes of their fellow-citizens, disgusting and blasphemous; that they will continue to swear the candidate to this oath of secrecy, under no less a penalty than that of having his throat cut across from ear to ear, his tongue torn out by the roots, and his body buried in the rough sand of the sea, at low-water mark, where the tide ebbs and flows twice in twenty-four hours; but that they will take care to explain to him that this only means he will rather die than reveal to any person under the canopy of heaven these secrets known to all the world; that his oath is not to interfere with his religion or politics, nor with any of his duties to his neighbor, his country, or his God. For thus speaks the mystic muse of Masonry:

And many a holy text around she strews,
To teach Masonic moralists to die.

Have I proved that the Entered Apprentice's *oath* is a breach of law, human and divine? that its *promise* is undefined, unlawful, and nugatory? that its *penalty* is barbarous, inhuman, murderous in its term, and, in its least obnoxious sense, null and void? If so, my task is done. The first step in Freemasonry is a false step. The Entered Apprentice's obligation is a crime, and, like all vicious usages, should be abolished.

JOHN QUINCY ADAMS.

TO WILLIAM L. STONE, ESQ.

QUINCY, 4 September, 1832.

Dear Sir:—On the 19th ult. I wrote you a letter containing some observations upon the volume of letters upon Masonry and Antimasonry, which you have done me the honor of addressing me It was confidential, and intimated my intention to pursue the subject hereafter. So far as it is connected with the presidential election now approaching, I abstain from all interference with it. But the abolition of Freemasonry in this Union is a *cause* which you have made your own, and which I trust you will not abandon.

In the seventh letter of your volume, in confirmation of the statement that the Masonic obligations are administered in very different phraseology in different places, you refer me to inclosed copies of the obligations of the seven degrees as they were given twenty-five years since in the lodge and chapter of an eastern city. You add among other things that these forms were introduced and adopted at Rochester, in the State of New York, when Royal Arch Masonry was introduced there. And you invite my attention to the difference between the Royal Arch obligation as contained in this manuscript and that in Bernard's book.

There is in the volume a reference to the note B, in the appendix. But *there* I find only an apology for the omission of this manuscript because it would have swelled the volume to a size beyond your intention.

If it would not give you too much trouble I should be obliged to you for a communication to me of this manuscript, which you can forward by the mail, and which will be returned to you as you may direct.

I am, very respectfully, dear sir,

Your friend and servant,

JOHN QUINCY ADAMS.

TO HIS EXCELLENCY, LEVI LINCOLN, GOVERNOR OF MASSACHUSETTS.

[EXTRACT.]

WASHINGTON, 1 February, 1832.

Dear Sir:—My Antimasonry has cooled down a little while objects less important but more urgent absorb my time and attention; but it has not been extinguished by the mental reservations of the twelve hundred certifiers to their own integrity, which I never thought of impeaching, nor has it been remarkably edified by the *ostensible* investigation of the committee of the Rhode Island legislature, or its results. I share in no spirit of Antimasonic *proscription*, if such there be; but if I had any right of person or property pending in a court of justice with an Entered Apprentice or a Knight Templar for my adversary, I should much disincline to see any man sworn upon my jury who had been present at the mur-

der and resuscitation of Hiram Abiff, and still
more to any one who should have crawled upon
all-fours under the living arch.   In other words,
I do hold as disqualified for an impartial juror, at
least between a Mason and an Antimason, any
man who has taken the Masonic oaths and ad-
heres to them, not excepting the twelve hundred
certifiers themselves.   With regard to church-fel-
lowship, I am not prepared to speak so particularly.   I am in church-communion with several
of the twelve hundred, and have perfect confidence in their integrity.   But I would challenge
them as jurors, between me and the Master Mason
who made oath that he had been twice present
with me at a lodge in Pittsfield; or between me
and the Master Mason who had the impudence to
vouch in my father as a patron of Masonry.

I have said that I share in no Antimasonic
proscriptions, if such there be; and I repeat the
assurance, that so far from approving or counte-
nancing their nomination of any candidate in
opposition to you, I did unequivocally disapprove
of that measure, and as far as I could dissuade
them from it.   I am happy to give you this
assurance, nor will I press further for the name
of him who attempted to induce in your mind a
different belief.   I have no doubt he was acting
under Masonic law as faithfully as the brethren

of the Royal Arch, who Morganized the bottom of Niagara River. *Agnosco fratrem.*

JOHN QUINCY ADAMS.

TO ALEXANDER H. EVERETT, ESQ., BOSTON.

[EXTRACT.]

QUINCY, 18 August, 1832.

With respect to conciliating the Antimasons in this commonwealth, though it is rather late for the National Republicans to begin, it may be better late than never. I most sincerely and heartily wish that they would. The National Republicans of this commonweath have not understood—they do not and I fear *will* *not* understand—the state of the Antimasonic question. About a year ago the grand lodge of Rhode Island published a formal *defense of Masonry,* in which they said they could not tell whether Morgan had been murdered or not, for *they knew nothing about it.* I have read a declaration published on the last day of the last year, signed by twelve hundred Masons of this our own state, who speak of a high excitement, which *had been* in the public mind, carried to it "by the *partial and inflammatory* representations of *certain offenses* committed by a

few misguided members of the Masonic institution
in a sister state." The National Republicans of
Massachusetts know nothing about *these certain
offenses;* but they have for two years past taken
most especial care to turn out of office every Antimason upon whom they could lay their hands, all
the while bitterly complaining of the persecuting
and proscriptive spirit of political Antimasonry.

The cause of Antimasonry must and will survive the next presidential election. And if the
National Republicans of Massachusetts really
wish for the co-operation of Antimasons, I have
no doubt they can obtain it. Whether they can
agree upon a ticket for the presidential election
now so near at hand, is doubtful in my mind; but
I take it for granted that for this time the National Republicans can carry their elections without
them. The Masonic declaration of last winter, to
which I have alluded, considers the Antimasonic
excitement as having subsided, and they certainly
did appear to have lost ground in this state, and
at least to have gained none in the states of New
York and Pennsylvania. There is now an apparent union of the two parties in New York, but
whether it will be cordial or successful is very
problematical. The National Republicans there
are more sanguine than the Antimasons, and

there are wounds between them not easily to be healed. You know how it is here.

Upon the subject of Antimasonry I have no suffered myself to be excited, although there has been no lack of provocations. But I *do* know something about the *Masonic murder* of Morgan, and the clusters of crimes perpetrated for the suppression of his book. I know something also of the laws, oaths, obligations, and penalties of Masonry, and I have not been unobservant of their practical effect, from murder under the sealed obligation, down to the prevarication of pretending that to have the throat cut from ear to ear *means* expulsion from the lodge. If the Masonic controversy were now raging in Cochin-China, and the name of Hiram Abiff had never been heard upon this continent, the subject would be worthy of investigation, as a philosophical inquiry into the mysteries of human nature. I have endeavored to consider it as a question upon the first principles of morals. I have sought for the facts from the Masonic as well as from the Antimasonic side, and have read Henry Brown, as well as Avery Allyn and David Bernard. Col. Stone's letters, which you have doubtless seen, were addressed to me, in consequence of inquiries which I had addressed to a brother Mason of his in Philadelphia, which were communicated to him.

Stone is a Knight Templar, and, as you know, a very ardent National Republican. His Masonic spirit lingers with him through his whole book, but he is an honest man,—unperverted even by the fifth libation,—and a bold one, or he never would have dared to proclaim the truths contained in those letters. I ask your particular attention to the letters from twenty-one to twenty-five inclusive, and to the forty-eighth, and I wish you would recommend the perusal of them to those of your National Republican friends, who are accessible to reason upon this subject. I abstain purposely from any public manifestation of opinion upon this topic, to avoid all appearance of interfering with the approaching presidential election.

Faithfully your friend,

JOHN QUINCY ADAMS.

TO RICHARD RUSH ESQ., YORK, PENNSYLVANIA.

QUINCY, 30 August, 1832.

My Dear Sir:—Since my letter of the third instant, I have not had the pleasure of hearing from you. In the interval I have been solicited with some urgency, on one hand by the National Republicans, and on the other by the Antimasons

of this commonwealth, to repair to their respective standards, which are not here the same
There is yet some obscurity with regard to the
result of the compromise, said to have taken
place in New York and Pennsylvania; and there
is no prospect of an agreement between them
here.

Of this I have had the opportunity to satisfy
myself, and it has confirmed my conviction of the
propriety of my abstaining from interference with
the elections. I have therefore declined attending as a delegate at the Antimasonic state convention, to be held at Worcester on the 5th of
next month, to make nominations for the offices
of governor and lieutenant-governor of the commonwealth, and of an electoral ticket for the
choice of president and vice-president of the
United States.

But while refraining from all agency in the approaching elections, I am, as a true and faithful
Antimason, *in search* of light. Now there are
three modes of lighting a lamp, with which I am
almost equally familiar. One at noon-day, with
a burning-glass, by the radiance of the sun ; one
in times of clouds and darkness with flint, steel,
tinder, and a match; and one either by night or
day, in sunshine or in shade, kindled at the light
of another lamp. In the analogy between the

worlds of matter and of mind, electioneering seems to me to light the lamp by the collision of flint and steel. But I, reserving that process for use when the others fail, or can not be applied, content myself for the present with lighting my lamp by the flame of another, or by the concentrated illumination from the source of light.

I have, therefore, since my return home, read with close and critical attention the volume of letters addressed to me by Col. Stone. This book was, if not composed, at least addressed to me in consequence of those letters, which about this time last year I wrote to Edward Ingersoll, and which he then communicated to Mr. Stone. They contained a specification of nine crimes, atrocious as any that can be committed by man, with *inquiries* whether they had not been committed in the transactions connected with the murder of Morgan, and whether the organized institution of Freemasonry, its corporate bodies of lodges, chapters, and encampments, were not accessory to all these crimes, before or after the fact.

Mr. Stone's book is the answer to these inquiries. He is, against the institution, the best of witnesses. He has taken ten degrees of Masonry, and is, in Masonic language, a worthy Sir Knight Templar. He has never renounced nor ever formally seceded from the institution. Long after the murder of Morgan he believed that no Masonic *lodge* had in any manner polluted itself with the guilt of his blood. But, as the editor of a respectable journal, he did not suffer his Masonic obligations to control his moral duties. He disdained to justify, to connive at, or to suppress the commission of crimes. His journal did give to the public statements of the facts as they became authenticated, and this soon brought him into collision with numbers of adhering Masons, and with the *grand lodge* of the State of New York. Then after a sharp altercation and bitter reproaches for his admission into the columns of his newspaper of *truth* against *Masonic murder;* and after an ineffectual struggle to save the grand lodge from the turpitude of an appropriation of money for the benefit of the western sufferers, he withdrew, and says he has never set his foot in a lodge-room from that day.

Col. Stone, I have said, is the best of witnesses against Masonry, for he is an upright, intelligent, and most *unwilling* witness. He testifies under the shackles of all his Masonic obligations, and with the knowledge that he is incurring the vindictive and unforgiving resentment of the craft. This is the destiny of every non-adhering Mason, and it places him in a position of no trifling or inconsiderable peril. His testimony confirms, far beyond any anticipation that I had formed, the extent to which the lodges, chapters, and encampments of the State of New York are implicated in the Morgan-murder crimes. It demonstrates beyond all possibility of reply, not only that nine crimes specified in my letter to Edward Ingersoll have been committed, but that lodges, chapters, and encampments have been accessory to every one of them, before or after the fact. It proves also that the crimes committed were more numerous than my specifications, and that several others should be added to the list. As you have Stone's book, I refer you to the letters from twenty-one to twenty-five inclusive, and to letter forty-eight, and will ask at your leisure for your thoughts on the *facts* there disclosed.

With a view to the ultimate object of Antimasonry, *the abolition of Freemasonry in these United States*, it appears to me to be an important point gained, if we produce on the public mind a full conviction that those crimes have been committed, and that *Masonry* is responsible for them.

The honest, adhering Masons turn away their eyes from the facts, and urge the people to do the same. The reason of this is that they can not look at the facts, and defend the institution, but they give thereby an immense advantage in the controversy to their adversaries. For an argument must be founded upon facts; he who has most perfect possession of facts, must have the firmest foundation for argument.

But after establishing the facts, first of the crimes committed, and secondly of the participation of many organized Masonic bodies in them, there is another point of view, to which it seems advisable to call the attention of the public to induce them to look at the institution *a priori*, to examine and analyze it, as it is in its nature. In a conversation with Col. Stone, after he had proposed to address the letters to me, but before he had begun the work, he was pleading, as he does in his book, for the institution as *he* had known and shared in it, and denied that he had ever taken the oath with the words "*murder and treason not excepted.*" I said to him that the first step of Masonry was a stumbling-block to me. That the Entered Apprentice's oath was vicious, and infected the whole institution. He has stated this observation of mine in his book, in terms I think rather stronger than those that I used. I have therefore written him two letters, with a full development of the sentiment which I did express to him, and of the reasons upon which it is founded. I have not written them for the purpose of present publication; and I inclose them to you, before transmitting them to him, and will be grateful to you for any remarks that may occur to you upon the perusal of them, after which I will ask you to return them to me. You will perceive that a concentration of legal, religious, and moral objection against the very first act of initiation to Masonry is, in truth, laying the corner-stone to the edifice of Antimasonry. This part of the system seems to me not to have been sufficiently canvassed. The adhering and seceding Masons have been disputing about single items in the Master Mason's, Royal Arch, and Templar's obligations, which are differently administered in different lodges, chapters, and encampments, while the vital question seems to me to be in the Entered Apprentice's oath, obligation, and penalty. The chemist who detects arsenic in a cup of coffee may inquire, for curiosity, whether it was mingled up with the powder of the berry, or poured into the boiling kettle; a motive of more intense interest to those who repair with the pitcher to the fountain should be to examine whether the poison has not been deposited there.

You will estimate the confidence which I repose in your candor as well as in your judgment when I add, that in submitting the inclosed letters to your examination I have not forgotten that you, like Washington and Warren, had once taken the Entered Apprentice's oath yourself.

Accept the assurance of

my respect and affection.

JOHN QUINCY ADAMS.

———

TO BENJAMIN COWELL, ESQ., PROVIDENCE, R. I.

WASHINGTON, 28 November, 1832.

Sir:—Your letter of the 22d instant, inclosing your address before the Antimasonic convention, held at Providence on the 2d instant, proposes a question of considerable difficulty, namely, by what means the institution of Freemasonry, with all its exceptionable properties, may be put down.

I answer, by the voluntary dissolution of the society, or by its extinction by the forbearance of others to contract its obligations.

I have hoped that the virtuous and intelligent members of the order, upon finding that all their secrets have been revealed and made public; upon perceiving the numerous atrocious crimes connected with the murder of Morgan, and to which their oaths, obligations, and penalties have given rise; and upon discovering the general obloquy into which the institution was gradually sinking, would frankly have abandoned it, of their own

accord. This expectation has not been fully
realized. But great numbers of Masons have
ceased to frequent the lodges; numbers of lodges
and chapters have suffered their charters to expire; and I believe the instances are now few in
which they swear a man upon the penalty of having his throat cut from ear to ear, to keep secret
from every human being, what every human
being, who will read the books of David Bernard
and Avery Allyn knows as well as the brightest
Masons of the land,— still, the majority of Masons do adhere to the craft, and refuse to give
up their idol. The only way to deal with them
is, to bring to bear upon them public opinion;
and that mode of treatment has been pursued
with regard to the disease, with considerable
and encouraging success.

I concur with you in the opinion that the administration of Masonic oaths, obligations, and
penalties ought to be prohibited by statutes of the
state legislatures, with penalties annexed to them,
not of cutting throats from ear to ear, nor of cutting the body in two by the middle, nor of opening the left breast and tearing out the heart and
vitals, nor of smiting off the skull to serve as a
cup for the fifth libation; but with good, whole-
some penalties of fine and imprisonment, adequate to their purpose of deterring every master,

grand master, grand king, or other dignitary of the sublime and ineffable degrees, from evermore polluting his lips with the execrable formularies, which have at length been dragged into light. Most cordially would I, were I a member of any state legislature in the Union, give my voice and vote for the enactment of such monitory statutes. But this can not be effected so long as Masonry controls the majorities in the state legislatures,— that is, so long as the people continue to elect, as members of the state legislatures, adhering Free-masons, or men who are neither Masons nor Anti-masons, or what you call *moral* Antimasons; men who disapprove Masonry, but are afraid of incurring Masonic vengeance by raising a finger or uttering a word against it; men whose virtue consists in neutrality between right and wrong, and who are willing to believe that to refuse their votes to a man because he is an adhering Free-mason is *persecution.* So long as the people con-tinue to constitute majorities of their state legis-latures of such men as these, so long will it be idle to expect any statutory enactment against Masonic oaths, obligations, and penalties.

It is, therefore, the duty of pure and disinterested Antimasonry to operate, as well as it can, upon public opinion; and one of the most effective modes of thus operating is the ballot-box. It is just and proper that every individual, honestly believing that the Masonic institution is an enormous nuisance in the community, which, if not voluntarily relinquished, ought to be broken down by the arm of the law, should resolve that he will vote for individuals, as members of the state legislatures, entertaining, upon this subject, the same opinions as himself, and for none other. If this resolution be just and proper for each individual separately, it is equally so for as many individuals collectively as can agree upon the principle. Far from being obnoxious to the charge of persecution, it is, perhaps, the mildest of all possible forms of operating upon public opinion—by public opinion itself. It is thus that the Antimasons have acted; first in the State of New York, where the Morgan murder has fastened upon the hand of Masonry a spot of blood, like that which the dream of Macbeth's wife paints upon hers, and which all the perfumes of Arabia can never sweeten; and subsequently in other states, including that of Rhode Island Thus far the principle of political Antimasonry has my hearty approbation; and in the diversity of opinion which still unhappily prevails on this question, it is a satisfaction to me that the dictate of my judgment coincides with that of a large majority of the inhabitants of my native town,

my friends and neighbors, and of a highly
respectable portion, if not a majority, of the constituents whom I have the honor of representing
in the congress of the United States.

With regard to the political course of the Antimasons in Rhode Island, I am not a competent
judge. To the cause of Antimasonry, I consider
the legislative investigation of the last winter as
having essentially contributed. It has substantially settled the question what the *oaths, obligations*, and *penalties* of Freemasonry *are;* it has
cut short all quibbling equivocation and attempts
to blast the credit of Avery Allyn and David
Bernard; it has given us these oaths, obligations,
and penalties in their naked deformity; it has
dragged the struggling savage into day, and has
shown us the last writhings of his Protean form,
in the impudent pretension that the death of a
traitor, in Masonic language, means the death of
a martyr. To the conclusions of the majority of
the committee of investigation, namely, that it
is the indispensable duty of the Masons to dissolve
their fraternity, I respond, Amen and amen;
though, when I read their report and observe the
process by which they reach them, I can not forbear an exclamation of astonishment at the novel
process of induction, by which their conclusion
slaps the face of all their premises.

I hope and trust that the Freemasons of Rhode Island will ultimately follow the advice of the committee of investigation, which so magnanimously waived the legislative right of exacting testimony to their secrets, and thus suffered the law of the land to cower before the law of Masonic secrecy. I thank the committee for having peremptorily exacted the real oaths, obligations, and penalties, as taken and administered in Rhode Island, and consider the result as having settled, in the mind of every reasonable and independent man, their nature and their character.

Respectfully, sir,

Your servant and fellow-citizen,

JOHN QUINCY ADAMS.

TO JAMES MOORHEAD, ESQ., MERCER, PENN.

WASHINGTON, 23 December, 1832.

Sir:—Mr. Banks, the worthy representative of your district, delivered to me your friendly letter of the 26th of last month. I have, since the commencement of the session of congress, regularly received the numbers of the *Mercer Luminary*, and have observed with pleasure the zeal and assiduity with which it disseminates the light of

Antimasonry. To that cause I am devoted, because I believe it to be the cause of pure morals and of truth. Until the murder of Morgan I had very little knowledge of the institution of Freemasonry, except as an occasional witness of its childish pageantry and the mock solemnity of its processions. These I believed to be harmless, and I gave willing credit to their boastful professions of benevolence and charity. Very soon after the Morgan catastrophe, however, the Masonic *obligations* were disclosed to me in the escape of Col. William King, from the pursuit of justice, in the territory of Arkansas. I saw their operation without being able to punish the offender or even judicially to authenticate the offense. King escaped by the connivance of Masonic obligations paramount to the laws of the land. He re-appeared afterward upon the theater of his guilt, and, as you know, died suddenly on the disclosing of facts which he had flattered himself were hidden from every person under the canopy of heaven, without the pale of Masonic oaths and penalties. Other evidences of the practical effect of Masonic obligations soon revealed themselves to me in the forms of *secret slander* and perjury. But of the multitude of atrocious crimes committed, first in the conspiracy which terminated in the murder of Morgan, and for five years afterward in baffling and defeating the laws of the state in their efforts to bring the murderers to justice, I had a very imperfect idea till the publication of Col. Stone's book.

There remained yet not any reasonable doubt, but some deficiency of evidence, with regard to the essential, inherent, and indelible viciousness of the Masonic obligations, in the solemn protestations of the adhering Masons, that those obligations were falsely represented in the books of Bernard and Avery Allyn; in the bold asseverations that no such oaths, obligations, and penalties existed; and in reiterated declarations, couched in delusive generalities, that *they* had never taken any oath or obligation inconsistent with their duties to their country or their religion, but always without disclosing what *were* the terms of those which they had taken. The investigation by a committee of the legislature of Rhode Island finally brought out the obligations of ten degrees, as avowed to be practiced in the lodges, chapters, and encampments of that state. It exposed them in their hideous deformity, and took from the defenders of Masonry their last refuge of prevarication.

It was to show them in their naked nature, divested of all sophisticated explanations, and all mental equivocations, that I wrote the four letters on the Entered Apprentice's oath, which you have republished in the *Luminary*. I am happy that they have met your approbation.

> I am, with much respect,
>> Your friend and fellow-citizen,
>>> JOHN QUINCY ADAMS.

——

TO EDWARD LIVINGSTON, ESQ.

WASHINGTON, 10 April, 1833.

Sir:—In the *National Intelligencer* of the 22d of April, 1830, there appears an address, there said to have been delivered by you, to the General Royal Arch Chapter of the United States, upon your installation to the high Masonic official dignity of their general grand high-priest.

In that address, after a feeling and elegant acknowledgment of the grateful emotions which you experienced on being apprized of the unexpected and unsolicited distinction which had been conferred upon you by your election to that office, and a pathetic allusion to that period of life when all worldly honors fade into the "sear and yellow leaf," you assign as your reason for accepting the dignity and the charge of presiding over an association in whose labors you had "for many

11

years retired from any participation," that your
refusal might have been " ascribed to an unmanly
fear of encountering the clamor raised against
our institution [of Freemasonry], or to a consciousness that the vile and absurd accusations against .
it were well founded. Either of these suspicions
[you added] would have injured not my character only, but that of the whole fraternity."

You further assigned an additional motive for
overcoming the reluctance suggested by the consciousness that your long retirement had rendered
you less fit to fill than many others, equally well
qualified in other respects ; and this motive was
your confidence in the Masonic skill and excellent
character of the worthy companion who was, at
the same solemnity, installed with you as your
deputy general grand high-priest.

After these ceremonial preliminaries, you proceed as follows :

"*Companions and Brethren :* For the first time
in the history of our country, persecution has
raised itself against our honorable fraternity. It
does not, indeed, as in other countries, incarcerate
our bodies, strain them on the wheel, or consume
them in the flames of the inquisition ; but its attacks are, to an honorable mind, as unjustifiable.
It assails our reputation with the blackest calumnies ; strives, by the most absurd inventions, to

deprive us of the confidence of our fellow-citizens; belies the principles of our order, and represents us as bound to each other by obligations subversive of civil order, and hostile to religion."

Mr. Livingston: In molding this personified image of persecution, did it never occur to you that the foul and midnight hag, who justly bears that name, is never to herself more deliciously occupied than in charging *persecution* upon others? In those Holy Scriptures, which it is your official duty to read and expound to your companions and brethren of the Royal Arch, it is related, that when your predecessor in the high-priesthood, Ananias, commanded that Paul should be smitten on the mouth, the apostle of the gentiles turned upon him and said, "God shall smite thee, thou whited wall; for sittest thou to judge me after the law, and commandest me to be smitten contrary to the law?" I will not imitate this exclamation of Paul, for which he himself apologized when informed that it was the high-priest to whom he spoke; but I will ask you, sir, to reconsider this charge of persecution, imputed by you in the face of the world, not indeed to any individual by name, but to a numerous and respectable class of your fellow-citizens in nine or ten states of the Union,—to all that class

of citizens known in the community by the de
nomination of Antimasons. I am one of them
myself. As respects myself I know—as regards
the whole party I firmly believe—that in the above
passage of your address you did them great
injustice. In charging them with calumny you
calumniated them yourself. In accusing them of
persecution, you are yourself the persecutor.

I will not say that on your part this persecution
and calumny were willful. You had for many
years retired from any participation in the labors
of the craft. If this fact is not very pregnant of
evidence, that, in your estimation, the labors of
the craft were, when you participated in them, of
a high order of public usefulness or private
beneficence, it exculpates you at least from all participation in labors of evil. You did not know
what new labors had, most especially in your own
native State of New York, and extensively else-
where, been ingrafted upon the old stock. You
did not know the additions which had been, in
many lodges and chapters, made to the whole
graduation of your oaths. The tree had not
borne all its fruits. The Morgan tragedy had
been enacted, and more than three years of impunity had, in evasion or defiance of the laws of
nature, of justice, and of the land, sheltered the
guilt of its perpetrators; but you did not know,

nor was there mortal out of the pale of your penalties who did know, the catalogue of *Masonic*
crimes which had been committed in affiliated
connection with that Masonic murder;—you know
them not to this day. Multitudes of them are,
and will ever remain, secreted under the seal of
the fifth libation, and under the obligation to conceal from every person under the canopy of
heaven, the secrets of a *worthy* brother,—murder and treason not excepted, or excepted at the
option of the swearer. More than a year after
your address was delivered the grand lodge of
Rhode Island published a defense of Masonry
against those same charges which they, like you,
pronounced persecutions and calumnies. Yet,
even then, they said that whether Morgan had
been murdered or not, they could not tell, *for they
knew nothing about it.* They knew nothing about
it! They knew nothing about the facts proved·
in the judicial tribunals of New York, not only
by clouds of witnesses, but by the confessions and
pleas of guilty of several among the conspirators
themselves. The grand lodge of Rhode Island,
one and all, knew nothing about all this, and yet
they published a defense of Masonry, and pronounced persecution and calumny, the denunciations of virtuous indignation against those very
judicially authenticated facts, about which they
declared that *they knew nothing.*

Sir, your address to your Royal Arch compan
ions had more of candor or more of discretion
You advised them that calumnies so absurd as
those uttered against you (the Masons) were best
met by dignified silence! And yet you did not
meet them by dignified silence; you pronounced
them from your exalted seat of general grand
high-priest of the order, black and absurd
calumnies, and you attributed them all to persecution.

But if I am bound to acknowledge the candor
and discretion of your advice to your brethren to
meet the charges against their institution with
dignified silence, I can not offer an equal tribute
of commendation to your consistency, when after
all your bitter complaints of calumny and persecution, you urge them to "be just, and reflect
how much cause for excitement has been given
by the outrageous abduction of a citizen dragged
from his family and friends, in the midst of a
populous state, followed up, *most probably*, by the
perpetration of a most atrocious murder."

You then remind them that "it was natural,
from all the circumstances of this most extraordinary and savage act, to believe that it was committed by Masons."

Sir, was it not committed by Masons?

"It was in human nature,—*unenlightened and*

prejudiced human nature,—to impute the cause of the offense to some secret tenet of the fraternity, and to involve them in the criminality of their guilty members."

Why the words *unenlightened and prejudiced?* Was not some secret tenet of the fraternity the cause of the offense? That tenet of the fraternity, secret at the time of the murder of Morgan, is secret now no longer. For the mere intention to reveal it, Morgan paid the penalty of his Entered Apprentice's oath; his book revealed it after his death. Its revelation was authenticated on the 4th of July, 1828, by the testimony, not of unenlightened and prejudiced human nature, but of the Le Roy convention of seceding Masons,— men who themselves had taken these oaths, and declared themselves subject to the penalties which had been inflicted by Masonic hands upon Morgan.

"It was natural that ambitious men should keep up the excitement, and direct it against political adversaries for their own elevation."

Perhaps it was. You, Mr. Livingston, are versed in the ways of ambition and ambitious men. You know their propensity to keep up excitements, and to direct them against political adversaries for their own elevation. You must know, you can not but know, that Masonry has been used by ambitious men for the same purposes. You must know that in many of the New York lodges the promise to promote a brother's political advancement was one of the recent additions to the Masonic obligations. You may and ought to know that wherever the spirit of Antimasonry has arisen, one of the first discoveries made by it has been that wherever a lodge or chapter has existed, at least three fourths of all the elective offices in the place were held by worthy brethren and companions of the craft, chosen by men, multitudes of whom knew not themselves the influence under which their votes were cast. You know, too, that the charge of ambitious and selfish motives is one of the most vulgar and most hacknied imputations of all ambitious rivals and competitors against one another. In condescending to use it yourself against the Antimasons, you certainly gave no additional dignity to it; and as a defense of the institution against Antimasonry, you might with advantage to yourself have remembered your advice to your brethren, and preferred to such a shield, the armor of dignified silence.

"And it was quite natural that men should be found simple enough not to see through their views, credulous enough to believe their absurd tales, or sufficiently unprincipled to propagate them, knowing them to be false."

This again may be true. Of simple, of credulous, and of unprincipled men, there are always numbers in every community, and they are the natural instruments of politicians of more ambition than principle. But, in this respect, as in many others, Antimasonry is and has been more sinned against than sinning. Simple and credulous men have, for example, been told by the general grand high-priest of the General Royal Arch Chapter of the United States, that the charges against the Masonic institution of having had some secret tenet, which was the cause of the murder of Morgan, were black and absurd calumnies, invented by persecution, and which none but fools and cullies could believe, and none but knaves would propagate. Simple and credulous men may believe these assertions of the general grand high-priest, because they are made by him, and because his character gives them the weight of authority. To simple and credulous men, the highest of all evidence is the authority of great names, and accordingly your own most plausible answer to the Antimasonic charges against your institution, is an appeal to the great and good men who have belonged and still belong to it.

But, sir, this is not sound reasoning to influence the minds of other than simple and credulous men. The question, permit me to say, upon the issue which I am about to take with you is not *who*—but *what*—not *who* have bound themselves by the Masonic oaths, obligations, and penalties, but *what* these oaths, obligations, and penalties are. *What* is their nature? and *what* have been their fruits?

Now, sir, I do aver that "the cause of the offense"—that is the murder of William Morgan and of a multitude of other crimes indissolubly connected with it,—was a secret tenet of the fraternity—secret then but no longer secret now. It consisted in the obligation and penalty of the *Entered Apprentice's oath.* It was the secret tenet of *initiation* to the Masonic institution.

This, sir, is the issue which I, an Antimason, tender to you, the general grand high-priest of the General Royal Arch Chapter of the United States. I call upon you, sir, in that capacity, to sustain the charge of persecution and calumny made by you in your address to your brethren and companions, upon your installation, against the whole body of Antimasons in the United States, and to sustain the institution over which you preside, against the charges which you pronounce persecuting and calumnious.

But this, sir, is not my whole or my ultimate purpose. I do conscientiously and sincerely believe that the order of Freemasonry, if not the greatest, is one of the greatest moral and political evils under which this Union is now laboring. I further believe that the primary and efficient cause of all this evil is that same rite of *initiation;* for as all the oaths, obligations, and penalties of the subsequent degrees are but variations, expansions, and aggravations of that primitive vice, let that be once abolished and all the rest must fall with it; knock away the underpinning, and the whole scaffolding must come to the ground.

With this address, I have the honor of submitting to you a pamphlet containing four letters on the *Entered Apprentice's oath.* You will perceive, sir, that they arraign that act of initiation upon five distinct charges, as contrary to the laws of religion, to the laws of morality, to the laws of the land.

Those letters have been now more than six months published. Their existence has not been noticed by any of the newspapers of the country under Masonic influence; but they have been very extensively circulated in pamphlets, and numerous editions of them have been issued in several of the states of the Union. They have of course attracted much of that benevolence and charity, in the construction of motive, for which the Masonic order is so conspicuous, upon the head of their author, but no attempt has to my knowledge been made to answer them. They were first published in the *Commercial Advertiser* of New York, and addressed to its editor, Col. William L. Stone, known to you as a distinguished companion of your order in the degree of a Knight Templar.

I have expected that some show of defense against the charges in those letters would have been made. The charges are grave,—they are specific,—they are made under the responsibility of my name. And now, sir, as no individual brother or companion of the craft has been willing to undertake its defense, I call upon you, as the general grand high-priest of the order in these United States, to undertake it. I call upon you the more freely, because, if the charges are true, there is a debt of justice and of reparation due from you to all the Antimasons of the United States. The charges are in part the same with those which you have pronounced absurd, calumnious, and persecuting. If, upon examination, you find them *true*, I expect from your candor an acknowledgment of your error; from your magnanimity, a retraction of your charges against the Antimasons.

I expect more. If, upon a fair examination of these charges against the *Entered Apprentice's*

oath, obligation, and penalty, you should find yourself unable to defend them before the tribunal of
public opinion; if you should, by the natural
rectitude and intelligence of your *enlightened and
unprejudiced* mind, come to the conclusion that
the first initiatory rite of Freemasonry is in its
own nature vicious, immoral, and unlawful; that
no mental reservation can excuse it; that no explanation can change its nature; that no plea of
nullity can purify the attainder of its bloody purport; then, sir, I expect that, as the general
grand high-priest of the order, you will immediately advise its abolition, or at least recommend
that it should never more be administered. I ask
not merely of the grand high-priest of Masonry,
but of the profound and eloquent and humane
legislator of the criminal code for Louisiana; I
ask of him the abolition forever of that brutal
penalty of death by torture and mutilation, for
the disclosure of senseless secrets; or rather, now,
of secrets proclaimed from every housetop of the
land. I say to you, in the language of the Roman
orator, in the sentiment of a heart congenial
with your own: "Hanc domesticam crudelitatem
tollite ex civitate; hanc pati nolite diutius in hac
republica versari; quæ non modo id habet in se
mali, quod civem atrocissime sustulit, verum
etiam hominibus lenissimis ademit misericordiam.

Nam cum omnibus horis aliquid atrociter fieri
videmus, aut audimus; etiam qui natura mitissimi
sumus, assiduitate molestiarum *sensum omnem
humanitatis ex animis amittimus.*" *

I propose to address you upon this subject
again. There is in the pamphlet herewith inclosed a fifth letter addressed to Benjamin Cowell,
of Rhode Island, containing my opinion in favor,
to a certain extent, of what has been called political Antimasonry. As this principle has had, and
must continue to have, a powerful influence upon
the policy and upon the history of this Union, it
will not be unworthy of your consideration in
your other capacity of secretary of state of these
United States. I shall endeavor to prove to
your conviction that your exhortation to the
brethren and companions of your order throughout the Union, but *under your jurisdiction, not to
be tempted to the slightest interference in political
parties,* has been and must be unavailing and
nugatory, that so long as you adhere to the administration of the Entered Apprentice's oath,

---

* Banish from our borders, suffer no longer to prey upon our vitals
this *home-bred* cruelty among a people hitherto renowned for the merciful treatment of their *foreign* foes. Its greatest evil is not this most
atrocious murder of a free citizen, but that it extinguishes the very
sentiment of compassion in the mildest hearts. For when our eyes
and ears are hourly tortured with the sight and recital of deeds of horror, they cease even in the tenderest natures to sympathize with human
calamity, *and the very sense of humanity is obliterated from our souls.*

your lodges and chapters must and will be political caucuses, and that Masonry will be the signal
for political proscription to one party, as Antimasonry has been and will be to the other.

I am, very respectfully, sir,
Your fellow-citizen,
JOHN QUINCY ADAMS.

TO EDWARD LIVINGSTON, ESQ.

PHILADELPHIA, 15 April, 1833.

Sir:—In a former letter I stated to you the
motives and purposes by which I was induced to
address you, as the presiding officer of the Masonic order in the United States, through the
medium of the press. They were—

1. To defend the Antimasons of the United
States from severe and unjust imputations and
charges against them, preferred by you in your
address to the brethren and companions of the
society upon your installation in your high Masonic dignity.

2. To make, distinctly, specifically, and under
the responsibility of my name, the charge against
the institution of Freemasonry, which you in that
address had pronounced a vile and absurd calum-

ny, instigated by a spirit of persecution, unjustifiable as arbitrary imprisonment or the tortures of
the inquisition, namely, that "the cause of the
offense," that is, of the murder of William Morgan, and of a multitude of other crimes connected
with it, was a secret tenet of the Masonic fraternity, consisting in the Entered Apprentice's oath,
obligation, and penalty—the first rite of initiation
in the Masonic order.

3.   To transmit to you four letters upon that
Entered Apprentice's oath, obligation, and penalty, published by me in November last, and intended to prove that this first rite of initiation to
the order of Freemasonry is, in its naked nature,
divested of mental reservation, stripped of the
authority of great names, and disarmed of the
shield of fraudulent explanation,—*vicious*, contrary to the laws of God, to the laws of humanity,
to the laws of the land.

4. To call upon you, as the head and chief of
the whole Masonic brotherhood of the United
States, to sustain your charges against the Antimasons,—to vindicate the purity, the humanity,
the lawfulness of the Entered Apprentice's oath,
obligation, and penalty,—or to advise and recommend to the companions and brethren under your
jurisdiction, *its abolition.*]

This last, sir, was my principal and ultimate

object in addressing you,—the *abolition* of that disgraceful initiatory act which continues the vital essence of Freemasonry.

I intended and intend no disrespect to you. Admiring your talents, concurring in many of your political opinions, and believing that in the discharge of your official duties in the service of the one, confederated North American people, you have at a critical moment of their Union, contributed much to its preservation, by dashing from their lips the deadly but Circæan cup of nullification and secession, my confidence in your character has been strengthened. Giving you the credit of bold resistance to dangerous political errors, and of intrepidity in the honorable undertaking of redeeming others from the same, I have been encouraged to hope that you will discern the pure and well-deserved honor which will assuredly await your name in after ages, if you shall avail yourself of that summit of Masonic dignity which you have attained, by prevailing upon the whole association to discard forever the use and administration of those horrible invocations of the name of a merciful God, as the witness to promises of secrecy to things no longer secret to any one, under penalties of death in every variety of form which a fury could devise, or a demon could consummate.

12

One of those oaths—that of the Royal Arch
Companion—it is your * special province, as the
grand high-priest of the order, to administer to
every Most Excellent Master, who, not satisfied
with this superlative excellence, still pushes forward in search of more light,—it is the seventh
of that series of blasphemies, or of calls upon the
name of God in vain, by which the Masonic
aspirant purchases the floods of light which pour
upon him from every successive degree. It is in
this degree that you turn that scene of awful
solemnity, the calling of Moses by God himself
in the burning bush, into a theatrical representation, and actually make your candidate take off
his shoes, declaring the place on which he stands
to be holy ground. This representation I know
is emblematic, and is explained by you to your
candidate so to be. The solemnities of admission
to the Royal Arch are deeply impressive, and
therefore the more exceptionable by their mixture

---

* It appears from Allyn's Ritual that it is not the high-priest, but the
principal sojourner of a Royal Arch Chapter, who administers the oath
and obligation to the team of candidates whom he leads by their halter
to the altar. But the high-priest gravely declares to them that an old
chest which he receives, *with great surprise,* from the principal sojourner,
is *the ark of the covenant of God.* He takes out of this chest an old book,
which upon beginning to read he finds to be "the book of the law,"
long lost, but now found, and he solemnly declares to the candidates
that "*the world is indebted to Masonry for the preservation of this sacred
volume.*" How edifying must this solemnity be to the ministers of the
gospel who take part in it!

in the same ceremonies with childish fables and
gross impostures. You commence with a fervent
prayer to God; you open the Royal Arch Chapter, and read to the three candidates for admission (for so many you must have) a great part of
the 139th psalm. You interrogate them, and bid
them travel three successive times, and on their
return you read portions of the 141st, 142d, and
143d psalms. You then order them to be conducted to the altar, and there you administer to
them the Royal Arch oath. This is the oath,
which, in many of the chapters of the State of
New York, pledges the candidate to conceal the
secrets of a Royal Arch companion, communicated to him as such,—murder and treason not excepted. It pledges him also to assist a brother
companion to extricate him from his difficulties,
whether he be right or wrong. In other chapters
the engagements are less onerous. They vary in
almost every chapter. In an authentic copy of
the manuscripts mentioned by Col. Stone in his
letters on Masonry and Antimasonry, one of the
promises of this degree is to support, protect, and
defend a Royal Arch Mason, *even with the sword
if necessity requires.* But in whatever form the
oath is administered, its promises, whether more
or less comprehensive or exceptionable, are all
made with invocation of the name of God; and

all under no less penalty than to have the swearer's skull smitten off, and his brains exposed to
the scorching heat of the sun. This, sir, is the
penalty under which you require of the candidate
for the Royal Arch degree to swear that he will
keep all the secrets of the order and of its companions and brethren, and that he will perform
the other obligations appertaining to that degree.
You deliberately pronounce, word by word,
causing the candidate to repeat them after you,
the words of this oath, promise, and penalty,
closing with the adjuration, So help me God, and
keep me steadfast to this my oath of a Royal Arch
Mason. And before he can be qualified to take
upon himself this obligation he must have had
six similar oaths administered to him, and have
pledged himself to them, so help him God, under
no less penalties than—

1. To have his throat cut across from ear to ear,
his tongue torn out by the roots and buried (his
tongue or his body) in the rough sands of the
sea, where the tide ebbs and flows twice in
twenty-four hours.

2. To have his left breast cut open, his heart
torn out and cast away to be devoured by vultures.

3. To have his body severed in two by the
midst, his bowels burned to ashes, and scattered to the winds.

The three succeeding penalties are of the same character, equally cruel and inhuman.

All these penalties William Morgan had incurred by writing the secrets and mysteries of the craft for publication. If it were possible to concentrate upon one human being the torture of them all, the agonies of that mortal would not be more prolonged or more excruciating than was the punishment inflicted upon William Morgan. He was seized by Masonic ruffians at noonday, hurried away from a dependent wife and infant children, by a warrant upon a false charge of larceny, taken out at thirty miles distant from his abode—taken out upon the day hallowed to the worship of God,—he was carried into another county, and discharged as innocent the moment he was brought to trial. Then forthwith arrested again for a debt of two dollars, imprisoned for two days, though he offered his coat in payment of the debt; finally discharged again in the darkness of night, by an impostor under the guise of friendship, and, immediately upon issuing from prison, seized again, under cover of the night, by concerted signals, between the man-stealers of the lodge and of the chapter—gagged to stifle his cries for aid, forced into a coach and transported, by changes of horses and carriages prepared at every change beforehand for his reception, one hundred and fifty miles, there lodged in solitary confinement within the walls of an old abandoned fortress, there detained five days and nights, under perpetual threats of instant death, subject to uninterrupted indignity and abuse—denied the light of heaven in his cell, denied the use of a Bible, for which he earnestly entreated, and finally, at dead of night, transported by four Royal Arch companions of the *avenging* craft to the wide channel of the Niagara River, and there sunk to the bottom of that river. Nine days were occupied in the execution of this Masonic sentence. At least three hundred worthy brethren and companions of the order were engaged as principals or accessories in the guilt of this cluster of crimes,—and *this*, Mr. Livingston, is "the offense," the "cause" of which I aver to be the *then* secret tenet of the fraternity, the oath, the obligation, and penalty of initiation to the mysteries of the craft.

I attribute them all to the Entered Apprentice's oath, because I consider that as the cause and parent of all the oaths, obligations, and penalties of all the subsequent degrees. My ultimate object in these addresses being to obtain, through your influence and recommendation, the voluntary relinquishment by the fraternity, in this Union, of these oaths and penalties, I have been desirous

of narrowing down the controversy to its simplest
point. I ask of you, and through you I petition
of the General Grand Royal Arch Chapter of the
United States to abolish the Royal Arch oath and
penalty; to require of all the chapters under your
jurisdiction to cease from administering that and
all other oaths tainted with the penalty of death,
forever; and this I trust and believe will induce
the lodges to follow the example of the chapters,
and abolish their oaths and penalties too, forever.

And when I charge the Entered Apprentice's
oath as the cause of the offense,—that is of the
kidnapping and murder of William Morgan,—I
only meet and repel your charge against the Antimasons, as persecutors and calumniators of your
fraternity, because they impute that offense to
that cause. But this is not *all* the offense of
which I impeach the Masonic penalties as the
cause. The abduction and murder of Morgan are
but two of a multitude of crimes connected with
that series of transactions of which they formed
a part, *all* of which I impute to the same cause.
There were crimes committed against Morgan
before his abduction and murder—crimes of equal
atrocity committed against his associate, Miller,—
crimes committed *after* the murder of Morgan, to
shield, and screen, and protect, and aid, and abet
its perpetrators,—crimes committed by Masonic

sheriffs in returning juries, — crimes committed
by Masonic witnesses, some in standing obstinately mute, and others in refusing to give the testimony required of them by the laws of the land,—
crimes committed by Masonic jurors in returning
false, or in refusing to return true verdicts. All
these I charge to the same cause; and not the
least among them is a false and calumnious imputation upon the character and good name of
your own immediate predecessor, in the office of
general grand high-priest of the Grand Royal
Arch Chapter of the United States, and then governor of the State of New York—an imputation
which embittered the last days of his life. It
must be known to you that one of the principal
conspirators against Morgan gave out among his
associates, to stimulate their faltering courage to
the deed of horror, that he had a letter from the
general grand high-priest declaring the Morgan
manuscripts must be suppressed, even at the cost
of blood; that such a letter, purporting to be
from Governor Clinton, was exhibited, and that
he, the governor of the State of New York, eminent and distinguished as he had long been, was
reduced to the humiliating necessity of directing
that an action of slander should be commenced to
vindicate his character before a judicial tribunal,
where Masonic witnesses have since been sen-

tenced to imprisonment for refusing to testify to
the truth. To refute this calumny upon Governor
Clinton was one of the honorable motives of
Colonel Stone for the publication of his letters
upon Masonry and Antimasonry. He has, in my
judgment, done it effectually; but he has admitted and shown that it was a calumny strictly Masonic,—a natural and congenial deduction from
the same oaths, obligations, and penalties which
sunk Morgan in the waters of the Niagara.

In the address to your companions and brethren
at your installation, which has been the occasion
of these letters to you, it was said that it would
be not more unjust and absurd to impute to the
Christian religion all the crimes which have been
committed in its name, than it is to charge the
institution of Freemasonry with the outrages of a
few misguided and infatuated members of the
craft. This argument is familiar to all the
defenders of Freemasonry, and has an appearance
of plausibility; but it is fallacious. All the crimes
committed in the name and under color of the
Christian religion, have been perpetrated under
false or erroneous constructions of its precepts.
There is nothing in the Christian religion to warrant them. But whenever and wherever those
false and erroneous constructions have been detected and exposed they have been exploded.

This is precisely the object of the Antimasons at this time, with regard to the errors and vices of the Masonic institution. They are to the order of Freemasonry what the Protestant reformers were to the Christian religion. Perhaps an analogy still more accurate may present itself to your mind between the letters of Blaise Pascal upon the morals of the order of Jesuits and those which I have now the honor of addressing to you upon the morals of Masonry. The tenets which in the name of the Christian religion have drenched the world in blood, were spurious; they formed no part of the religion itself. The tenets of the order of Jesuits, detected and exposed by Pascal, were not universally held by the members of that institution; they formed no part of the constitution of the society, and were disclaimed by its brightest ornaments. The order of Jesuits was a religious community. The whole system of their establishment was founded upon the precepts of Christ. They read the Bible as assiduously, and with devotion as profound and sincere, as animates the grand high-priest of the Royal Arch, upon the admission of a triad of candidates to that Masonic degree. And yet the order of Jesuits has been abolished by the head of the Catholic Church himself for holding tenets and adopting practices inconsistent with good morals.

But the vices of the Masonic institution are not false and erroneous constructions of precepts ill understood and susceptible of different meanings. They are vices inherent in the institution itself, and not corruptions foisted upon it. Cruel and barbarous as was the penalty inflicted upon Morgan, it was no more than he had at least seven times sworn to endure for violation of his Masonic oaths. His murderers, those of them who survive, are still *worthy* brethren and companions of the craft. Not one of them has ever been·expelled from lodge, chapter, or encampment. They have been, on the contrary, cheered with the sympathies and relieved from the funds of the grand lodge and grand chapters of New York. You perceive, then, that whatever analogy there may be between the crimes committed by the corruptions of the Christian religion, and those resulting from Masonry, the inferences to be drawn from it all speak trumpet-tongued for the abolition of the Masonic oaths and penalties.

In concluding this letter I am bound to make my acknowledgments for a poetical parody of its predecessor, which I have seen in the newspaper called the *Globe*, and by which I see that you are disposed to treat the subject with pleasantry. Well, sir, so be it. The *Globe* is generally considered as your *political* organ. In that country, which it is said you are about to visit, you may, perhaps, at your hours of leisure and recreation, occasionally frequent the first dramatic theater in the world, and there be entertained with exhibitions, not of Moses in the burning bush, but of some of the masterpieces of the human mind in the form of comedies of Moliere. You may chance to see, among the rest, a personage upon the stage speaking to his servant and about to give him an order, when the servant interrupts him by the inquiry whether he is speaking to his *coachman* or to his *cook*. A similar question occurs to me with regard to your poet laureate. Is it one of your charioteers of the department of state, or a scullion of the kitchen? In either event, I commend this epistle to the inspiration of his muse;—and as for you, sir, when the time for seriousness shall return, and you shall incline to justify yourself from the charge of unjust accusation against multitudes of your fellow-citizens, or to vindicate from still more serious charges he oaths, obligations, and penalties which it is among your official Masonic functions to administer,—when you shall return to the grave and solemn and religious character of the general grand high-priest, I shall hope to hear from you, in verse or prose, in the *Globe* or the *Intelligencer*, at your option, but in your own person, and with the signature of your name.

I am, in the meantime,

Very respectfully, your fellow-citizen,

JOHN QUINCY ADAMS.

TO EDWARD LIVINGSTON, ESQ.

QUINCY, 1 May, 1833.

Sir:—The Entered Apprentice's oath, obligation, and penalty, upon which I took to animadvert, in the four letters to Col. William L. Stone, a copy of which was transmitted to you, with the first of these letters to yourself, was in the terms of that obligation as furnished by the officers of the grand lodge of Rhode Island themselves, to the committee of the legislature of that state, appointed to investigate the charges against the institution which had been made since the murder of Morgan, and which they and you pronounce calumnious. The obligations themselves had never been authenticated by the authority of adhering Masons, until they were produced by the officers of the grand lodge and grand chapter, at the peremptory requisition of the legislative committee. They were generally considered by Masons as constituting essential parts of the mysteries of the craft, and included strictly within the promise never to write, print, cut, carve, paint, stain or engrave them. In the practice of the chapters and lodges, the oaths are all administered by rote, and pass by tradition alone. This is of course the cause of the differences in the phraseology of the oaths as administered by different persons. It is one of the great inherent vices of the institution. It affords constant opportunity and frequent temptation to every chapter and lodge to make additions to the promises pledged by the recipient of each degree.

The manuscript obligations furnished by the grand chapter and grand lodge of Rhode Island were drawn up and reduced to writing for the occasion. The grand lodge had previously published a *defense* of Masonry, stoutly denying that there was anything in the Masonic obligations contrary to religion, morals, or the laws of the land; but carefully abstaining from any statement of what they were. They had used that notable device of explaining the penalty of death *for* revealing the secrets of the craft, or of any of its members, as meaning only a promise to suffer death *rather* than reveal them. They had expounded and explained and denied the several parts and parcels of the Masonic obligations, till they had made them all as innocent as their lambskin aprons. They had especially denied, with abundance of indignation, that *they* had ever administered or taken the oath to conceal the secrets of a brother Mason—"murder and treason not excepted." These words, or others equivalent to them, are stated, in Elder Bernard's Light on Masonry, and in Avery Allyn's Ritual, to form a part of the Royal Arch obligation. They are certified as such by the convention of seceding Masons, held at Le Roy, on the fourth of July, 1828, twenty three of whom had taken this oath; and they have since been attested by adhering Masons, upon trials before judicial tribunals in the State of New York. They are not in the Royal Arch obligation reported by the grand chapter of Rhode Island; but in the Master Mason's obligation, reported by the grand lodge. Among the promises of admission to that degree are the following words,—"That I will keep a brother's secrets as my own, when committed to me in charge as such, murder and treason excepted." This, of course, is a pledge of immunity, for all other crimes, but it does except murder and treason. So said the grand lodge of Rhode Island. Yet even in that state, Nathan Whiting, an attorney and counsellor at law, who had taken the degree in the lodge at East Greenwich, and had been master of that lodge, testified that in the Master's degree, after "murder and treason excepted," the

usual form was to add "*and that at my option*"—
and what the difference is between that, and
"murder and treason not excepted," I leave as a
problem in morals for Masonic casuists to solve.

In the seventh of Col. Stone's Letters upon Masonry, page 66, referring to the disagreement in
the phraseology of the obligations, as given in
different places, he makes mention of a manuscript
then in his possession, containing copies of the
obligations of the several degrees, as they were
given twenty years before in the lodge and chapter
of an eastern city—copied from the manuscript of
a distinguished gentleman who had been master of
the lodge and high-priest of the chapter.   The
forms, says Col. Stone, are the same that were
used in that city for a long series of years; and
when Royal Arch Masonry was introduced *into
Rochester, in the State of New York, these forms,
from these identical papers, were then and there introduced and adopted.*

There is at this passage a reference to a note in
the appendix, stating it to have been the original
intention of Col. Stone to insert all the obligations
contained in that manuscript, in his text; but that
he was compelled to suppress them from the un-
foreseen extent of his work.   He observes that
neither of the obligations in the first three degrees, in those manuscripts, is more than half as

long as those disclosed by Morgan, and in common use. He further adds that these manuscripts give a more sensible and intelligible, and a less exceptionable account of the seven degrees of Masonry, than any other work he had seen; and he concludes by observing that *when Morgan was at Rochester, these papers were there, and already written to his hands.*

It is to be regretted that Col. Stone did not adhere to his first intention of publishing these obligations, or rather that he did not insert the whole manuscript in his appendix. I have obtained it from him, and annex hereto the three obligations as there recorded, of the Entered Apprentice, [the Fellowcraft, and the Master Mason. It will be found upon examination, that although truly represented by him as perhaps not more than half so long as the same obligations in Morgan's and Bernard's books, they lose nothing of pith and moment by the retrenchment of words. They were the forms used at Rochester, and no other Masonic institution in the state was more deeply implicated in the tragedy of Morgan's kidnapping and murder, than that same chapter at Rochester. Now, in the Entered Apprentice's oath of this manuscript, the promise is expressly and explicitly to keep and conceal the secrets of Masons as well as Masonry. The penalty is the

13

same as that reported by the grand lodge of Rhode Island, but in the lecture to the candidate on his admission there is in the manuscript an *explanation* of the meaning of the *penalty*, which not only utterly falsifies the explanation of the Rhode Island Masons, so strangely accepted and countenanced by the majority report of the legislative investigating committee, but proves that the murderers of Morgan understood but too well the real character of the obligation.

In this Entered Apprentice's lecture, the candidate, after going through the forms of admission, is examined by the master, upon interrogatories with regard to the meaning of all the ceremonies through which he has passed. Upon giving the account of his admission at the door, the following, word for word, are the questions put to him by the Master, and his answers:

Q. "What did you next hear?"

A. "One from within, saying with an audible voice, Let him enter."

Q. "How did you enter?"

A. "Upon the point of a sword, spear, or other warlike instrument, presented to my naked left breast, accompanied with this expression, Do you feel?"

Q. "Your answer?"

A. "I do."

Q. "What was next said?"

A. "Let this be a prick to your conscience, a shield to your faith, *and instant death in case you revolt.*"

Yes, sir, this is the explanation given to the Entered Apprentice, at the time of his admission to the degrees, of the penalty under which he binds himself by his oath—this was the formula used in *Connecticut* more than twenty-five years since, and thence introduced into Rochester, in the State of New York. Who shall say that the murderers of Morgan misunderstood the import of the Entered Apprentice's obligation?

And in this same manuscript of the forms of admission used at Rochester, the following, word for word, are clauses of the Master Mason's obligation:

"I furthermore promise and swear, that I will attend a brother barefoot, if necessity requires, to warn him of approaching danger; that on my knees I will remember him in my prayers; that I will take him by the right hand and support him with the left, in all his just and lawful undertakings; that I will keep his secrets as safely deposited in my breast, as they are in his own, *treason and murder only excepted*, AND THOSE AT MY OPTION; that I will obey all true signs, tokens, and summonses, sent me by the hand of a Master Mason, or from the door of a just and regular Master Mason's lodge, if within the length of my cable-tow."

This was the form of admission to the Master Mason's degree, at Rochester, when the chapter at Rochester decided that Morgan had incurred the penalties of his obligations, and sent out their signs, tokens, and summonses accordingly.

These were the oaths which every Master Mason admitted at the lodge in Rochester, had taken. All this he had "most solemnly and sincerely promised and sworn with a full and hearty resolution to perform the same without any evasion, equivocation or mental reservation—under no less penalty than to have his body cut across, his bowels taken out and burnt to ashes, and those ashes scattered to the four winds of heaven; to have his body dissected into four equal parts, and those parts hung on the cardinal points of the compass, there to hang and remain as a terror to all those who shall presume to violate the sacred obligation of a Master Mason."

Col. Stone, in his seventh letter, page 67, says, that in his apprehension the words, "*and they left to my own election,*" are an innovation, and that he has not been accustomed to hear the obligation so conferred. The words in his own manuscript are "and those at my option;" fewer words, but bearing the same meaning. They were no innovation at Rochester.

The only words in this obligation which need any explanation, are the words *cable-tow*, and they are always so explained as to give them a definite meaning. The rest are all as explicit as language can make them, and they are taken with a broad and total disclaimer of all evasion, equivocation or mental reservation. So they were taken at Rochester, and so they are recorded in the old manuscript of Col. Stone.

You are a classical scholar, sir, and you doubtless remember the humorous remark of Cicero, in his dialogue on the nature of the gods; that he could not conceive how one Roman Haruspex could look another in the face without laughing. I find it difficult to conceive how you, performing the functions of a master of a lodge, as among the duties of a grand high-priest you may be required to do—how can you look in the face of a man after administering to him such an oath as this, without shuddering. But we have not yet done with the old manuscript of Col. Stone.

After the ceremonies of admission to the degree of Master Mason are completed, and the recipient has been invested in his new dignity, he is conducted to the master of the lodge in the east, there to hear from him the history of the degree.

There, sir, with equal regard for historical truth
and reverence for the Holy Scriptures, you mingle
up the building of Solomon's Temple, as recorded
in the Bible, with the murder of Hiram Abiff by
three Tyrian Fellowcraft, Jubela, Jubelo, and Jubelum, as preserved in the chronicles of Masonic
mystery.   You relate them all as solemn truth of
equal authenticity, and in the manuscript now before me, the story goes that after the murder of
Hiram Abiff was consummated, King Solomon
was informed of the conspiracy, and ordered the
roll to be called, when the three ruffians were
missing.   Search " was made after them, and they
were found by their dolorous moans, in a cave.
Oh, said Jubela, that my throat had been cut
across, &c. [repeating the whole penalty of the
Entered Apprentice's obligation] before I had
been accessory to the death of so good a master.
Oh, said Jubelo, that my heart had been torn out,
&c. [repeating the whole penalty of the Fellowcraft's obligation] before I had been accessory to
the death of our master.   Oh, said Jubelum, that
my body were cut across, my bowels taken out
and burnt to ashes, &c. [repeating the whole penalty of the Master Mason's obligation] before I
had been the death of our master Hiram Abiff.
They were then taken, and sent to Hiram, king
of Tyre, who executed on them the several sen-

tences they had invoked upon themselves," *which have ever since remained "the standing penalties in the three first degrees in Masonry."*

This, sir, is the history of the Master Mason's degree, which was delivered by the master of the lodge at Rochester to every individual received as a Master Mason. This was the explanation given to him of the obligation assumed by him, immediately after the administration of the oath. This is in substance the explanation which you, the reporter of a criminal code to the legislature of Louisiana must give to every Master Mason whom you receive, of the penalty of the oath which you administer to him in the name of the ever-living God — without evasion — without equivocation — without mental reservation.

And will you say, sir, as the grand lodge of Rhode Island have said, that these penalties mean no more than that the swearer, who invokes them upon himself, will *rather* die like Hiram Abiff, than reveal the secrets of Masonry? Is it Hiram Abiff in this story who pays the *penalty* of violated vows? Is it Hiram Abiff who invokes these penalties upon himself? The Entered Apprentice, the Fellowcraft, and the Master Mason, invoke upon themselves the penalties of their respective degrees. The Entered Apprentice is told that he enters the lodge on the point of a naked sword pricking his breast, to remind him of *instant death in case of revolt;* and the Master Mason is told that the penalties *executed* upon Jubela, Jubelo, and Jubelum, have ever since remained *the standing penalties in the three first degrees of Masonry.*

And now, sir, what are we to think of high-priests, and Royal Arch chapters, and grand masters, and grand lodges, who after taking and *administering* in secret these oaths, with these penalties, for a long series of years, when their real character has been proclaimed by the voice of midnight murder from the waters of Niagara in tones to which the thunders of her cataract are but as a whisper—when their unequivocal import has been divulged, to the amazement and disgust and horror of all pure, unsophisticated minds; what are we 'to think of high-priests, and grand kings, and most illustrious Knights of the Cross, who face it out in defiance of the common sense and common feeling of mankind, that there is nothing in these oaths and penalties inconsistent with the duties of those who take and administer them, to their country or their God? The manuscript from which I now give to the world the three obligations of the Entered Apprentice, of the Fellowcraft, and of the Master Mason, is upon the testimony of Col. Stone, a Knight Templar and a man of unimpeached integrity, *masonry in its most mitigated and least exceptionable form,*— it was the masonry of Connecticut more than twenty-five years since and for many years before —it was the masonry of Rochester at the time of the murder of Morgan.

I have yet more to say to you, sir, on this subject, nor shall I be discouraged from continuing to address you upon it by your observance of a "dignified silence." If my letters are not read by you, there are those by whom they will be read, I trust, not without effect. If the presses under your jurisdiction, Masonic or political, refuse their columns to the discussion of Masonic morals, when the grand high-priest of Masonry is the secretary of state of the Union, it may serve to illustrate the subserviency of the periodical press to Masonry—but your address to your companions and brethren at your installation as the grand high-priest of the Royal Arch of this Union, is not the perishable effusion of a day. It is a state paper for history, and for biography—for the present age and for the next—it shall not be lost to posterity—it shall stand as a beacon to future time—the admiration, or at least the wonder of other generations.

JOHN QUINCY ADAMS.

TO EDWARD LIVINGSTON, ESQ.

QUINCY, 23 May, 1833.

Sir:—The position which I have undertaken to prove, beyond all possibility of rational denial, is, that the "cause of the offense," that is, of the murder of William Morgan, and of a multitude of other crimes associated with and subsequent to that act, was the oath of initiation to the Masonic institution, with its appended penalty.

Had Morgan ever taken any other oath than that of the Entered Apprentice, he would, after *writing* his Illustrations of Masonry, have been liable to the penalty which he suffered—even before they should be published. Like Jubela, Jubelo, and Jubelum, he had invoked the penalty upon himself; he suffered nothing more than the penalty which he had been assured had been executed upon them; nothing more than what he had been warned had been the standing penalties of Freemasonry from the time of the building of Solomon's Temple.

All the obligations are assumed, with invocation of the penalty of *death*, upon him who takes the oath of admission to each of the several degrees; pronounced with his own lips, and with a solemn appeal to God, disclaiming all evasion, all equivocation, all mental reservation.

Such is the law of Masonry.

Shall I cite to you, sir, from your able and eloquent report to the legislature of Louisiana, the powerful argument against the infliction of death upon *any* criminal for the commission of *any* crime whatsoever? The whole argument is well worthy to be read and studied, by every person conversant with the administration or enactment of criminal law, and of the deep consideration, especially of the brethren and companions of the craft. But the introduction to it is so peculiarly appropriate to the purpose of these addresses to you, that I take the liberty of presenting it to you in your own words.

"I approached the inquiry into the nature and effect of this punishment (of death) with the awe becoming a man who felt most deeply his liability to err, and the necessity of forming a correct opinion on a point so interesting to the justice of the country, the life of its citizens, and the character of its laws. I strove to clear my understanding from all prejudices which education or early impressions might have created, and to produce a frame of mind fitted for the investigation of truth and the impartial examination of the arguments on this great question. For this purpose I not

only consulted such writers on the subject as were
within my reach, but endeavored to procure a
knowledge of the practical effect of this punishment on different crimes in the several countries
where it is inflicted. In my situation, however,
I could draw but a limited advantage from either
of these sources; very few books on penal law,
even those most commonly referred to, are to be
found in the scanty collections of this place, and
my failure in procuring information from the
other states, is more to be regretted on this than
any other topic on which it was requested. With
these inadequate means, but after the best use
that my faculties would enable me to make of
them; after long reflection, and not until. I had
canvassed every argument that could suggest
itself to my mind, I came to the conclusion THAT
THE PUNISHMENT OF DEATH SHOULD FIND NO PLACE
IN THE CODE WHICH YOU HAVE 'DIRECTED ME TO
PRESENT."

Now, sir, I ask of you, as the grand high-priest
of the General Grand Royal Arch Chapter of the
United States, to make to the chapters and lodges,
to the companions and brethren under your jurisdiction, that some recommendation to abolish the
penalty of death, which with such deep and affecting solemnity you did make, in reporting a code
of criminal law to the legislature of Louisiana.

The argument of which I have here given only the introductory paragraph embraces a very large portion, nearly one half, of your report on the criminal code. In the system reported with it, murder, and joining an insurrection of slaves, are made punishable with hard labor for life. At the close of this letter I annex several other extracts,* as well from the report as from the preamble to the penal code reported with it, indicative not only of your deliberate and solemn opinions, adverse to the punishment of death in all cases whatsoever, but of the abhorrence which you must feel at heart, for those brutal mutilations of the body which constitute the penalties of *every* Masonic obligation.

It is not, Mr. Livingston, for the poor purpose of bringing against you a charge of inconsistency before the tribunal of public opinion, that I address these letters to you, and call earnestly upon you to make this recommendation. I would, if possible, speak to your heart. I would say, you have recommended, you have urged by appeals to the best feelings of our nature, to the supreme legislative authority of your state, the total abolition of the penalty of death,—the reformation of everything cruel, indecorous, or vindictive in her code of criminal law. You are at the head in

---

* These extracts are here omitted.

these United States of a private association of
immense power,—co-extensive with the civilized
world,—knit together by ties of strong prevail-
ment even when *secret*, scarcely less efficacious
when divulged. When secret, they were riveted
by pledges to the penalty of death and mutilation
in a multitude of forms, given in the name of
God, and varnished with an imposture of sanctity
by being mingled up with the most solemn testi-
monials of Holy Writ. Even now, when your
secrets are divulged, when your obligations and
penalties have been exposed in their naked and
undeniable nature, when you, *dare not* attempt
to vindicate or defend them, when the attempts
of your brethren to explain them have been
proved fraudulent and delusive, when your only
resource of apology for using them is that they
are null and void—words utterly without meaning, yet you still persevere in adhering to them as
the ancient landmarks of the order. Ask yourself, sir, not whether this is *consistent* with your
report and criminal code of Louisiana, but whether it is worthy of your character—of your stand
in the face of your country and of mankind; of
your reputation in after time; and if it is not and
can not be, why should you not take the occasion
of the high dignity which in this association you
have attained, to propose and to promote its ref-

ormation? to divest it of that which, so long as
it continues, can never cease to shed disgrace upon
the whole order; of that which can not even be
repeated without shame?

You have taken no public notice of these letters
in your own name, nor have I been particularly
solicitous that you should. Had you ventured to
assume the defense of the Masonic oaths, obligations, and penalties—had you *presumed* to commit
your name to the assertion that they can by any
possibility be reconciled to the laws of morality,
of Christianity, or of the land, I should have
deemed it my duty to reply, and to have completed the demonstration before God and man that
they *can not.* Of the multitude of defenses of Masonry, which have been obtruded upon the public
since this controversy arose, not one has dared to
look these obligations in the face, and assert their
innocence. Abuse upon the Antimasons for denouncing them—impudent denials of their import, so long as a remnant of the ragged veil of
secrecy rent by the seceders, could yet be drawn
over their nakedness—false and fraudulent *explanations* of their meaning when disclosed beyond
all possibility of denial, and mystical and mysti-
fied declarations of inflexible adherence to them
under the name of the *ancient landmarks* of the
institution—these have been the last resources,
the forlorn hopes of the Masonic obligations.

And this inflexible adherence to these *ancient landmarks* is again recommended to the chapters and lodges under your jurisdiction by the General Royal Arch Chapter of the United States, of which you are the high-priest, at their triennial meeting in Baltimore last November. At that meeting you were re-elected to the dignity which you had held from the time of your address to the companions and brethren of the order at your installation in April, 1830. A letter from you was read at that meeting, apologizing for your absence from it, and perhaps for the better accommodation of the grand high-priest, that meeting was adjourned to be held again in November, 1835, at the city of Washington.

There is a point of view in which I believe this subject to be deeply interesting to the people of this Union, upon which I have hitherto said nothing, and upon which I do not wish to enlarge. The president of the United States is a brother of the craft, bound by its oaths, obligations, and penalties, to the exclusive favors, be they more or less, of which they give the mutual pledge. That in the troubles and difficulties which within the last seven years have befallen the craft, they have availed themselves of his name, and authority, and influence to sustain their drooping fortunes, as far as has been in their power, has been a matter of public notoriety. A sense of propriety has restrained him from joining in their processions, as he has been importunately urged by invitations to do, but he has not withheld from them his support. It is not my intention to comment upon the operation of the Masonic obligations, upon the two most recent elections to the presidency of the United States, or upon the official conduct of the president himself in relation to the institution or its members. But whoever will impartially reflect upon the import of the Masonic obligations, and upon the public history of the United States for the last ten years, must come to the conclusion that no president of the United States ought ever to be shackled by such obligations, or under the self-assumed burden of such penalties. They establish between him and all the members of the institution, and between him and the institution itself, relations not only different from but utterly incompatible with those in which his station places him with the whole community. That the president of the United States is not at this moment an impartial person in the question between Masonry and Antimasonry, nor between Masons and Antimasons, has been fully authenticated, by something more than the effusions of your scullions in the *Globe.* He is not impartial. How can he be impartial after trammeling himself with

14

promises, such as those which are now unequivocally authenticated before the world?

And you, Mr. Livingston, secretary of state of
the United States, are at the same time grand
high-priest of the General Grand Royal Arch
Chapter of the United States; and all the Royal
Arch chapters of all the states of this Union are
under the jurisdiction of that over which you preside. Are you impartial in the question between
Masonry and Antimasonry? Are you, or can you
be impartial in any question which can arise
between Masons and Antimasons? You commenced your official duties as grand high-priest,
by a sweeping denunciation of all the Antimasons
in the Union. The Antimasons were then a great
political party. They are so still. You brought
against them what I have proved to be a most
unjust accusation. Are you impartial between
them and their adversaries? Has human nature
changed its properties since one of them was by
a profound observer said to be, to *hate* those whom
you have injured, "odisse quem læseris?" How
far distant from such a denunciation of Antimasonry as that with which you gratified your companions and brethren at your installation, is the
dismission for Antimasonry of an officer of the
United States, dependent on you for his place?
Is it as far as the department of state from the

general post-office? In all the trials before the judicial courts of the State of New York, to which the abduction and murder of Morgan has given rise, the efficacy of the Masonic obligations upon sheriffs, jurors, and witnesses to warp them from their duty to their country has been lamentably proved—what security can the country possess that they will not operate in the same manner upon a secretary of state, or a president of the United States? Were the Masonic obligations equivocal in their character, were they even susceptible of the explanations which have been attempted to be given of them, the undeniable fact, that they have been understood and acted upon according to their literal import, by great multitudes of Masons, to the total prostration of their duties to the laws of their country, would be a conclusive reason for abolishing them altogether. For if the obligations are of a nature to be differently understood by different persons, their consistency or inconsistency with the laws of the land must depend upon the individual characters of those who have assumed them. Bound by the same oaths, some of the witnesses and jurors on the Masonic trials in New York have given their testimony and true verdicts, while others have obstinately refused their testimony to facts within their knowledge, and denied their assent to verdicts upon the clearest proof. It has been judicially decided in the states of New York and of Rhode Island that a person under Masonic obligations must be set aside as disqualified to serve upon a jury in cases where one of the parties is a Mason, and the other is not. From the letter of his obligations he can not be impartial, and although some Masons may understand them otherwise, neither the court, nor the party whose rights and interests are staked upon the trial, can have any assurance that the trial will be fair. The same uncertainty must rest upon the administration of executive officers. If the president of the United States and the secretary of state are bound by solemn oaths and under horrible penalties to befriend and favor one class of individuals in the community more than another, the purposes for which those offices are instituted must be frustrated; a privileged order is palmed upon the community, more corrupting, more pernicious than the titles of nobility which our constitutions expressly prohibit, because its privileges are dispensed and enjoined under an avowed pledge of inviolable secrecy. In many of the New York chapters, the promise to promote the *political* preferment of a brother of the craft, over others equally qualified, was one of the Royal Arch obligations to which the companion was sworn upon

the penalty of death. How far such an obligation would influence the official conduct of a
president of the United States, it is impossible to
say ; but not more impossible than for that officer
to fulfill the obligations of such a promise and to
perform his duties with impartiality.

At the time when you delivered the address
upon your installation as grand high-priest of the
general grand chapter, Antimasonry had already
existed upwards of three years. It was an extensive political party, although then in a great measure confined within the limits of the State of New
York. You denounced it in no measured terms.
Had the charges which you openly brought against
it been true, every individual within the scope of
your denunciation must have been an unworthy
citizen and a dishonest man. Such has been the
tone of all the defenses and defenders of Masonry,
from that day to this. If the Masonic obligations were understood in all ordinary times not to
interfere with the religion or the politics of individuals, how can it be possible to preserve this
nominal exception when Masonry itself has become the most prominent object of political dis-
sension? As a political party, the Antimasons of
the United States are, at this day, probably more
numerous than the Masons. In several of the
states, the most important elections turn upon

that point alone. The Antimasons openly avow the principle of voting for no other than Antimasonic candidates. How is it possible for the Masons to preserve themselves from the political bias, prompting them to repel Antimasonry? They have in fact no such equanimity. They never fail to bring forward a candidate of their own when possible; and when they find it impracticable, they unite with any party, whatever may be their aversion to it, and however obnoxious its politics, to exclude the Antimason.

In your letter to the General Grand Royal Arch Chapter of the United States, of the 26th of November, 1832, apologizing to them for not attending at their meeting, then about to be held at Baltimore, you said thus: "You know (notwithstanding the allegations of our enemies) that the duties we owe to our country are paramount to the obligations of Masonry, or to the indulgence of fraternal feelings." Now, sir, my appeal is to the very principle here asserted by yourself. I aver that your duty to your country is violated by the administration of the Masonic oaths and obligations under penalties of death, invoked in the name of God—penalties multiplied beyond those of the most sanguinary code that ever disgraced human legislation, and for offenses which the supreme law of the state can not recognize as the most trifling of misdemeanors.

At that triennial meeting of the General Grand Royal Arch Chapter of the United States, a committee was appointed "to take into consideration the present situation of our [the Masonic] institution, and recommend such things and measures as they in their wisdom may consider expedient and necessary."

The report of that committee, and the resolutions proposed by them, and adopted by the General Grand Chapter of the United States, were the immediate occasion of these letters to you. This circumstance may account, in part, for what appears to have surprised some of your friends—that I should *now* hold you accountable for an address delivered so long since as April, 1830. That was your declaration of war against the Antimasons. In November, 1832, you still proclaimed them to be *your enemies*, and the General Grand Royal Arch Chapter, in full triennial meeting, repeated with renewed and aggravated denunciations, all your erroneous charges against them. Upon that report, and upon the resolutions with which it closed, I shall in my next letter submit to the consideration of the public some observations.

JOHN QUINCY ADAMS.

TO EDWARD LIVINGSTON, ESQ.

QUINCY, 12 June, 1833.

Sir:—From the official published report of the proceedings of the General Grand Royal Arch Chapter of the United States, at their triennial meeting at Baltimore, last November, it appears that a communication was made to that meeting from the M. E., Nathan R. Haswell, G. II. P. (meaning grand high-priest) of the grand chapter of Vermont, together with accompanying documents, and that this communication and the accompanying documents were referred to a committee which is denominated one of the most important committees then appointed, and they were instructed to take into consideration the present situation of the Masonic institution, and to recommend such things and measures as they in their wisdom might consider expedient and necessary.

The first remark that invites attention here, is, that this meeting was composed of individuals all belonging to different states of this Union, some of them occupying stations of power and dignity in their several states. The chairman of the committee to whom this communication was referred, and who made the report upon which I am to comment, is a member of the executive council of the commonwealth of Massachusetts, elected from a county exceedingly divided upon the questions between Masonry and Antimasonry—elected at the same time another was excluded from the same office, who, though an ardent National Republican and a sufferer by proscription from office by the present national administration, was discarded for a slight, real or suspected, taint of Antimasonry.

Here, then, is a member of the council of the State of Massachusetts, elected expressly in opposition to the Antimasonic party of the county of Bristol in that state, representing the Grand Royal Arch Chapter of Massachusetts, at a general convention of all the Royal Arch chapters of the United States, to which is referred a communication and documents from the Grand Royal Arch Chapter of Vermont.

That the report of a committee of which this gentleman was the chairman should be marked with strong resentment against the Antimasons of Vermont was to be expected. Political Antimasonry has been more successful in Vermont than in the county of Bristol in Massachusetts.

The report, therefore, states that it appears from the appeal published by the Masons in Ver-

mont in 1829, that various presses have been
established in that state as vehicles of slander
and malignity against the adherents of Masonry.

This is precisely a repetition of the language
of your address at your installation in April, 1830.
It is certainly not a correct representation of
facts, and it contains itself a slanderous imputation upon a majority of the people of the State of
Vermont.

Now, sir, for a far more rational and accurate
history of Antimasonry as it existed in the State
of Vermont in the years 1829 and 1830, I refer
you to a pamphlet entitled "Masonic Penalties,"
published in August, 1830, by William Slade,
now a member elect of the House of Representatives of the United States from that state.

In this pamphlet you will see that Mr. Slade
commenced the publication of his essays on the
Masonic penalties on the 7th of April, 1830, a
very few days before your installation and the
delivery of your address. You have probably
never seen those essays, for it appears to be one
of the maxims of Masonry, while denouncing as
slander, malignity, and persecution, every im-
peachment of the institution, to "*know nothing
about*" the real serious charges against it. It is
therefore highly probable that you know nothing
about Mr. Slade's essays on Masonic penalties.

And I take it for granted that the committee of the General Grand Royal Arch Chapter of the United States, who reported this bitter denunciation against the Antimasons of Vermont, knew no more about it than you do. I will hazard a conjecture that among the *documents* transmitted by the grand high-priest of the Grand Royal Arch Chapter of Vermont, and upon which the committee made their report, it would be a vain search to look for Mr. Slade's essays upon the Masonic penalties. "Dignified silence" was the rule to be observed with regard to them; and yet, sir, attempts were made to answer them. It is so far from being true that presses were set up in Vermont as vehicles of slander and malignity *against* the adherents of Masonry, that the editor of the Vermont *American*, who begun the publication of Mr. Slade's essays, suspended them after the third number, under the terror of Masonic vengeance; and Mr. Slade was compelled to publish the remaining numbers in an extra sheet. Yet the columns of the Vermont *American*, when closed against Mr. Slade, were opened to the defenders of Masonry, and two writers, under the signatures of "Common Sense of the Old School," and of "Senex," vainly attempted to refute the unanswerable arguments of his first three numbers. Mr. Slade replied, but was obliged to resort to the pages of a *free press*, one of those defamed by the report of the committee of the General Grand Royal Arch Chapter of the United States. Mr. Slade published in a pamphlet, under the responsibility of his name, his own essays, and those of his adversaries; and this procedure was in the same spirit of fairness and candor which marked his whole management of the controversy. I recommend to you the serious and attentive perusal of the pamphlet, for if it should serve no other purpose than to preserve you and the General Grand Royal Arch Chapter of the United States from the reiteration of insult and slander upon the people of a highly respectable state of this Union, it will have a just claim to your grateful acknowledgments—insult and slander upon the people of Vermont, who by their votes at the last presidential election, as well as by their suffrages at two succeeding elections for the executive officers and the state legislature, have signally vindicated the cause of Antimasonry. To this result it is obvious that Mr. Slade's essays upon the Masonic penalties did, in an eminent degree, contribute. It was impossible that they should fail to produce their effect upon the minds of an intelligent and virtuous people. These essays carry with them internal and irresistible evidence in refutation of the charge against the Antimasonic presses of Vermont, proffered by the committee of the General Grand Royal Arch Chapter of the United States. The essays on the Masonic penalties are not less remarkable for their moderation, delicacy, and tenderness to the adherents of Masonry, than for the close and pressing cogency of their arguments against the institution. They charge not the adherents of Masonry, but Masonry itself, with the murder of Morgan, and all its execrable progeny of crimes.

The report of the committee proceeds to state that the members of the grand lodge of Vermont, and other Masons in the state, to the number of nearly two hundred, published, in 1829, an appeal declaring that *they* as Masons had been charged—

1. With being accessory to the abduction of William Morgan.

2. With shielding Masons from just punishment for crimes they might have committed.

3. With exercising a Masonic influence over legislative, executive, and judiciary branches of the government.

4. With tampering with juries.

5. With exerting an improper influence for the political preferment of the brotherhood.

6. With various blasphemous practices.

7. With causing the death of a distinguished Mason.

8. With sanctioning principles at variance with religion and virtue.

9. With the assumption of a power to judge individual Masons by laws known only to the fraternity, and to inflict punishments corporally, even unto the pains of death.

Of each and all of these charges they affirm in the most solemn manner that they were entirely guiltless.

Now the error which pervades the whole of this declaration consists in this: that the individual Masons who volunteer this plea of not guilty, apply gratuitously to themselves the charges which the Antimasons bring against the institution to which they belong, and to its initiatory obligations and solemnities. The charges are against the plain, unequivocal import of the *laws* of Masonry. The charges are that those laws do in their own nature lead to and instigate the commission of all those crimes, and that they *have* led to and instigated the perpetration of them. Two hundred Masons of Vermont declare themselves guiltless of all these charges. There are perhaps two thousand Masons in the state,—suppose the two hundred appellants to be not guilty; that surely no more proves the innocence than it does the guilt of the remaining eighteen hundred. Had the Masons of Vermont been desirous of making up a *real* issue between themselves and the Antimasons, they should have said, We have been charged with administering and taking oaths and obligations, with multiplied penalties of death, which lead into the temptation of all those crimes, and which have led to the commission of them, and we have been urged to abolish these oaths, obligations, and penalties.

There is another error in this statement of the charges against themselves, to which the appellants pleaded not guilty, evidently suited to evade the real question at issue. Their charges are couched in general and indefinite terms, prepared for the purpose of meeting them with positive denial, by the mental reservation of their own misconstructions. They say, for example, that they have been charged with various blasphemous practices. Now what do they mean by blasphemous practices? Blasphemy, by the common law, and by some of the statutes of the states, is an indictable crime—and it is defined by Blackstone to be the denial of the being or providence of God; or contumelious reproaches of our Savior, Christ; or profane scoffing at the Holy Scriptures, or exposing it to contempt and ridicule.

Now, sir, if before the disclosure of William

Morgan, at the ceremonies of initiation to the several degrees of Masonry, the grand high-priests of the Royal Arch chapters, and the masters of lodges, instead of consciously hiding their heads in secrecy; if you, sir, as the sovereign master or most excellent prelate of an encampment, as the grand high-priest or principal sojourner of a chapter, or as the master of a lodge, had exhibited in public theatrical representations of the murder of Hiram Abiff, of Moses and the God of heaven in the burning bush, and of drinking the fifth libation from a human skull, with an invocation by the drinker of all the sins of him whose skull formed that cup, upon his own head; if in the presence of your fellow-citizens, you had uttered, as equally grave and solemn truth, a narrative compounded one half of quotations from Holy Writ, and the other half of the senseless and brutal mummeries of Masonry, would you have been surprised if the next morning a grand-jury of your county had presented you for blasphemy? Could you have imagined anything more calculated to bring reproach and contempt and ridicule upon the name of God and upon the Holy Scriptures? If any one of the ministers of God whom you allure into the bosom of a charitable institution, by admitting them gratuitously to its promises and its rewards, should tell his people from the pulpit that Hiram Abiff, the widow's son, was master of a lodge of Masons at the building of Solomon's Temple; that he was murdered by three Fellow-crafts, named Jubela, Jubelo, and Jubelum; that those three Fellowcrafts had suffered the penalties which they had invoked upon themselves, and that ever since that time those same penalties had been the standing penalties in the three first degrees of Masonry, would there be one hearer of that minister of Christ beyond the reach of the cable-tow but would pronounce him guilty of provoking contempt and ridicule upon the Scriptures?

Why, sir, if the pastor of a Christian church should bind up Gulliver's Travels between the Old and New Testament of his Bible, and read indiscriminately from the whole, the gospel, epistle, or collect of the day, what opinion would his auditory form of his piety or his morals? And yet there is much of truth and much of moral instruction in Gulliver's Travels. Far, far more of wisdom in the philosophers of the flying island of Lagado, than in the bungling metamorphosis of Hiram, the Tyrian brass-founder at the building of Solomon's Temple, into a Master Mason, or in the " butcheries which would disgust a savage " executed upon the three Tyrian Fellow-

15

crafts, and which you require of the candidates for admission to the three first degrees, to invoke upon themselves.

These are the practices which some of the ardent and zealous Antimasons of Vermont may possibly have qualified as blasphemous. I am not willing to consider them as such. That very secrecy under which they are performed, and which otherwise constitutes one of the most powerful objections to the institution, may perhaps relieve it from the charge of blasphemy. The intention is not to provoke contempt and ridicule upon the Scriptures, although the effect of them, as dramatic fictions, must often be to produce it. When John Milton published his Paradise Lost, Andrew Marvell declared that he for some time misdoubted his intent :

> That he would ruin
> The sacred truths to fable and old song—

And he adds—

> Or if a work so infinite be spanned,
> Jealous I was that some less skillful hand,
> Might hence presume the whole creation's day,
> To change in scenes, *and show it in a play.*

That which the penetrating sagacity and sincere piety of Andrew Marvell apprehended as an evil which might result even from the sublime

strains of the Paradise Lost, is precisely what the
contrivers of the Masonic mysteries have effected.
They have travestied the awful and miraculous
supernatural communications of the ineffable Jehovah to his favored people, into stage plays.
That Word, which in the beginning was with
God, and was God; that abstract, incorporeal,
essential, and ever-living existence; that eternal
presence without past, without future time; that
BEING, without beginning of days or end of years,
declared to Moses under the name of I AM
THAT I AM, the mountebank juggleries of
Masonry turn into a farce. A companion of the
Royal Arch personates Almighty God, and declares himself the Being of all eternity—I AM
THAT I AM. Your intention in the performance of this ceremony is to strike the imagination
of the candidate with terror and amazement. 1
acquit the fraternity, therefore, of blasphemy.
But I can not acquit them of extreme indiscre-
tion, and inexcusable abuse of the Holy Scriptures. The sealed obligation, the drinking of
wine from a human skull, is a ceremony not less
objectionable. This, you know, sir, is the scene
in which the candidate takes the skull in his hand
and says, "As the sins of the whole world were
laid upon the head of our Savior, so may the sins
of the person whose skull this once was, be

heaped upon my head in addition to my own; and
may they appear in judgment against me, both
here and hereafter, should I violate any obligation in Masonry or the orders of knight-
hood which I have heretofore taken, take at
this time, or may be hereafter instructed in, so
help me God;" and he drinks the wine from the
skull.

And is not this enough? No. The Knight
Templar takes an oath containing many promises
—binding himself under no less penalty than to
have his head struck off and placed on the highest spire in Christendom, should he knowingly or
willingly violate any part of his solemn obligation of a Knight Templar.

Mr. Livingston, is this a fitting obligation for
a *Christian man* to take or to administer? Can
you, can any man, be surprised if some of the
Antimasons of Vermont have mistaken it for
blasphemy? When the Masons of Vermont, or
when the Grand Encampment of the United
States shall feel sufficient confidence in their own
integrity to meet the real charges against the institution face to face, let them not resort to the
refuge of secrecy, as a hunted ostrich hides his
head in the sand—let them frankly acknowledge
the dramatic exhibition of the burning bush, and
the mystical cup of the fifth libation, and give

their definition of blasphemy from which these practices shall be pure.

And these remarks apply equally to the declarations of the Masons in Connecticut, and of the twelve hundred in Massachusetts. The report of the committee of the General Grand Royal Arch Chapter says that these declarations were made with apparent sincerity of heart, that they *denied* the charges against them [the Masons], "and universally cast themselves and their cause upon the good sense of the country, for a calm, dispassionate, and enlightened verdict."

And here the report of the committee rested the statement respecting the condition of Masonry in Vermont, Connecticut, and Massachusetts. The meeting of the General Grand Royal Arch Chapter was held at the close of November, 1832. The committee was raised to report upon the *present* condition of Masonry—and they report a declaration of two hundred Masons in Vermont in 1829, and a declaration of twelve hundred Masons of Massachusetts in 1831.

Mr. Slade's essays upon the Masonic penalties were published in Vermont in 1830, a year after the appeal of the two hundred Masons. The charters of incorporation of the Masonic lodges in Vermont were revoked by the legislature of that state in 1831. An Antimasonic governor and council, and Antimasonic electors of president and vice-president of the United States, were elected in 1831 and 1832—the last within one month before the meeting of the General Grand Royal Arch Chapter of the United States. These were all significant indications of the verdict passed by the people of Vermont upon the appeal of the two hundred Masons of 1829. But upon all these, the committee of the Grand Royal Arch Chapter of the United States observe a "dignified silence." Like the Rhode Island grand lodge, with regard to the kidnapping and murder of Morgan by Royal Arch Masons, *they knew nothing about it.*

The declaration of the twelve nundred Masons of Massachusetts was published in December, 1831. In September, 1832, less than three months before the meeting of the General Grand Royal Arch Chapter of the United States, a state Antimasonic convention was held at Worcester, at which an address was adopted containing a counter declaration to that of the twelve hundred. A committee of that convention tendered to the grand lodge and grand chapter an issue upon thirty-eight specific allegations against the Masonic institution, to be tried in any form best adapted to establish truth and expose imposition. And what was the answer of the twelve hundred

Masons who had made the declaration? "Dignified silence." What was the answer of the grand lodge and grand chapter of Massachusetts? "Dignified silence." And what the report of the committee of the Grand Royal Arch Chapter of the United States, on the [then] *present* condition of the Masonic institution? "Dignified silence." The twelve hundred Masons of Massachusetts, like the two hundred Masons of Vermont, make a statement of charges which they can safely deny,—assume them as the charges of the Antimasons against them, deny them, and then put themselves upon the country. When the Antimasons tender them a direct issue, upon specific charges, equally serious and explicit, the twelve hundred—the grand lodge, the grand chapter— all *stand mute*, and the report of the committee of the General Grand Royal Arch Chapter of the United States, upon the *present* condition of the Masonic institution, goes back one, two, and three years to tell of the declarations of Masons in Massachusetts and in Vermont. But as to any Antimasonic refutation of those declarations, the committee *knew nothing about it.*

The report of the committee of the General Grand Royal Arch Chapter of the United States was therefore an incorrect representation of the state of the Masonic institution, so far as concerned the states of Massachusetts and Vermont, nor was it more accurate in its reference to the state of Masonry in Rhode Island.

JOHN QUINCY ADAMS.

————

TO EDWARD LIVINGSTON, ESQ.

QUINCY, 23 July, 1833.

Sir:—You have seen in my last letter, the statement made by the committee of the General Grand Royal Arch Chapter of the United States, at their meeting in November last, of the then PRESENT CONDITION of the Masonic institution, in the states of Vermont, Massachusetts and Connecticut. You have seen that to exhibit this *present condition* of the craft, the report of the committee traveled backward in the race of time, one, two, and three years, to the declarations of their own innocence, by certain Masons of those states, the exclamation of Macbeth to Banquo—"*Thou canst not say I did it!*" But that upon the more recent events—the revocation of the Masonic charters in Vermont, the successive issues of the popular elections in that state and the thirty-eight specific charges against Masonry tendered by the committee of the Antimasonic convention at

Worcester, to the presiding officers of the Grand Royal Arch Chapter of Massachusetts and of the grand lodge; upon all this, the committee of the General Grand Royal Arch Chapter of the United States observed a profound and "dignified silence." And yet, sir, that issue of thirty-eight charges had been tendered on the eleventh of September, 1832—nearly nine months after the declaration of the twelve hundred Masons of Massachusetts, and less than three months before the meeting of the General Grand Royal Arch Chapter of the United States at Baltimore.

Now, sir, was not the presiding officer of the Grand Chapter of Royal Arch Masons of Massachusetts, to whom this issue was tendered, the identical chairman of the committee of the General Grand Royal Arch Chapter of the United States, which made this report on the then *present* condition of Masonry in the United States? And if he was, upon what principle admissible in a narrative of realities, could a report upon the *present condition* of Masonry in the United States, go back *three years* for declarations of Masonic innocence, and overlook or totally suppress the recent and actually present charges of Masonic guilt, which must have been yet sounding in the ears of the chairman of the General Grand Royal Arch Chapter who made the report? Is not the chronology of Masonry as peculiar to itself as its logic?

The committee upon the present condition of Masonry in the United States proceeded further to report, that from certain documents which had been, *for a long time* before the public, it appeared that very different measures in relation to the subject had been adopted in the State of Rhode Island; and so the committee reporting upon the *present* condition of the institution, chose to resort only to documents which had been a long time before the public. They say,

That in Rhode Island, "a memorial emanating from an Antimasonic convention, held in December, 1830, charging the grand lodge and other Masonic bodies with violations of the constitution and the laws of the land, was formally presented to the legislature of the state, and the grand lodge, in reviewing that memorial, challenged the strictest scrutiny, and offered the greatest facilities to an investigation of all their concerns;" but that "it seems, however, that after the most laborious and patient investigation of the subjects referred to in the memorial by an able and impartial committee, the lodges were sustained by the legislature of the state, and were *virtually* and triumphantly acquitted from all the charges which had been brought against them."

And who would imagine that within two months after this representation of the present condition of Masonry in Rhode Island, the legislature of that state did, by unanimous assent in both houses, enact a law, prohibiting the administration of all extrajudicial and of course of all Masonic oaths, upon no less penalties than a fine of one hundred dollars for the first offense, and political disfranchisement for the second? This was the first result of that investigation, which the committee of the General Grand Royal Arch Chapter consider as having issued so triumphantly for the lodges and chapters of Rhode Island.

They pronounce the investigating committee of the Rhode Island legislature "able and impartial." Of their ability no question will be made; but where did the reporter of the Grand Royal Arch Chapter of the United States find the evidence of their impartiality? Was it in the report of the majority, or in that of the minority of the investigating committee? Was it in the exclusion by the majority of the committee, of the very memorialists who had brought the charges against Masonry before the legislature, from all participation in the investigation? Was it in the bargain made by the chairman of the committee with the Masonic dignitaries of the state, that if they would give their obligations, they should not be questioned about their secrets?—a bargain made without the knowledge or consent of at least one member of the committee—a bargain to which the Masonic authorities held the committee of the legislature so strictly, that they repeatedly refused to answer questions most pertinent to the investigation, appealing to the chairman himself for the performance of his promise, that they should not be required to disclose any of their secrets. Is that the impartiality of a legislative investigation of charges of crimination?—first to exclude those who make the charges, from all participation in the process of inquiry—and then to contract with the parties accused, that they shall be privileged to refuse answering upon everything which they choose to keep secret. This was the course of proceeding of this impartial committee.

You are too well acquainted with the prevailing politics in the legislature of Rhode Island, at the time when this committee was appointed, not to know, that the main object of its appointment was to put down Antimasonry in Rhode Island. The resolution for appointing it was prepared by the chairman, but was offered by another member. In urging the passage of the resolution, both these persons indulged themselves in bitter invectives against the Antimasons, and the report of the majority of the committee carries upon every page the most conclusive internal evidence that the purpose for which the committee was raised, was to screen the Masonic institution and brotherhood from the investigation which had been demanded by the Antimasonic memorial, and to substitute in its place a colorable examination, upon which the Masons should answer just so much as should suit themselves, and fall back upon their obligations of secrecy whenever they should think a disclosure adverse to their interests.

The proceedings of the majority of the committee were conformable to the principles with which they entered upon the performance of the service assigned to them. The examination was so conducted that the Masonic witnesses answered just so far as they thought proper, and when a question was put, which from very shame they loathed to answer, they appealed to their agreement with the chairman, and set the inquiry at defiance.

The committee stated in their report that, aware of the scruples of the Masonic witnesses about disclosing their Masonic secrets, which they had promised not to disclose, they "resolved unanimously that they would require the Masons to communicate to them fully, their Masonic oaths or obligations, and to answer all questions which should be asked respecting them—those obligations not being considered as part of their secrets"—but "as to their signs, and tokens, and words, contrived to enable Masons, and none others, to enter lodges and to distinguish one another from those not Masons, *a majority* of the committee believed that the public *would have no curiosity about them*, and that it would not be a profitable or creditable employment for the committee to *endeavor to pry into them.*"

Admirable impartiality! Unlawful and immoral *secret* rites and ceremonies, was the first and foremost of all the charges against Masonry, from the sinking of their victim in the waters of the Niagara River. The supreme legislative authority of the state are called upon to investigate the subject. They appoint a committee for that purpose. The committee, possessed of the whole authority of the state to command testimony and elicit the whole truth, begin by excluding the accusers from all participation in the inquiry, and then bargain with the accused to ask no questions about their secrets, if they will but divulge what they themselves consider as no secret at all.

I do not propose to follow the majority of the committee through the mazes of their most extraordinary report. The report of Mr. Sprague, the member of the committee whose views differed from those of his colleagues, and the authentic report of their proceedings by Benjamin F. Hal-

lett and George Turner, have shown in full relief
the meaning of the word *impartiality*, as exempli-
fied by the committee and their chairman who
drew up their report. And yet, so far was the
committee entitled to the praise of impartiality, that they came unanimously to the conclusion
that the institution of Freemasonry *ought to be
abolished*, and the report concludes with an earnest
and eloquent exhortation to the Masonic fraternity
to abandon it.

Is it not very remarkable that the report to the
General Grand Royal Arch Chapter of the United
States, upon the *present* condition of Masonry,
which so highly approves this report of the Rhode
Island investigating committee, takes not the
slightest notice of this their opinion and exhortation? The Grand Royal Arch report affirms that
upon the report of the Rhode Island investigating
committee, "the *lodges were* SUSTAINED by the
legislature of the state." *Sustained!* this "able
and impartial" committee says:

"It can not be doubted that the lodges and
chapters in that part of the state [of New York]
had it fully in their power to have detected and
brought to justice many of the criminals concerned in the abduction of Morgan, if not those
concerned in his murder. And yet we do not
find that they have expelled a single member, or

made any manner of inquiry about them.   Can it be denied that by such conduct those lodges and chapters have implicated themselves in the *guilt of those transactions*, and made themselves responsible for it?   And not they alone are implicated.   *The higher Masonic authorities, to whom they are subordinate and accountable, are equally implicated and responsible.*"

The higher authorities, to whom the chapters in that part of the State of New York are subordinate and accountable, are, the grand chapter of the state, and the General Grand Royal Arch Chapter of the United States.   Yes, sir, in this passage of the Rhode Island "able and impartial" investigating committee's report, the very chapter of which you are the high-priest, the General Grand Royal Arch Chapter of the United States, is implicitly charged with being implicated and responsible for the guilt of the murder of Morgan.   How comes it, sir, that the committee of the General Grand Royal Arch Chapter of the United States, reporting upon the present condition of Masonry, and expressly referring to this report of the investigating legislative committee f Rhode Island, should have overlooked entirely this charge against the Grand Royal Arch Chapter of the United States itself?   How dared that committee to affirm that, as the result of that investigation, the lodges were sustained by the legislature of the state? The report of the Rhode Island investigating committee expressly charges the grand chapter of New York, and the General Grand Royal Arch Chapter of the United States, with being implicated in and responsible for the murder of Morgan, and the atrocious transactions connected with it; and the report of the General Grand Royal Arch Chapter of the United States calls this a triumphant acquittal of the lodges of Rhode Island!

Permit me, sir, to present to your consideration two more extracts from the same report of the majority of the Rhode Island investigating committee:

"The old forms of the oaths, which are still adhered to, are extremely improper. It is true that the construction which the Masons put upon them in this state [Rhode Island] renders them harmless, but that is by no means the natural construction of the language itself. The oaths taken by themselves, without being corrected and controlled by the addresses and charges, are, according to the terms, of them, clearly criminal. And can it be proper to take obligations, the different parts of which are in direct collision with and contradiction to each other, and yet the whole to be sworn to.

"But it is an insurmountable objection to those oaths that they are liable to a construction which renders them in the highest degree criminal and dangerous; and that such a construction has actually been put upon them by Masons, and has been productive of the most dreadful consequences."

The following is the concluding sentence of the report:

"This committee can not but come to the conclusion that the Masons owe it to the community, to themselves, and to sound principles, now to discontinue the Masonic institutions."

To what a desperate extremity must the committee of the General Grand Royal Arch Chapter of the United States have been reduced for matter to report upon the present condition of Masonry, when they were willing to accept and represent this as a triumphant acquittal of the Rhode Island lodges and chapters!

Yet this was a report of a committee so partial to the Masonic fraternity, that, invested with the entire legislative power to investigate their institution, they did in fact abdicate their legitimate rights and powers, by a bargain with the Masons, to screen them from the exposure of their most odious ceremonies. They accepted and countenanced a fraudulent explanation, and pretended construction of the penalties of the Masonic oaths. Fraudulent, as every Master Mason must know who at his reception is told that the penalties are, and have been from the building of Solomon's Temple, the same penalties which were *executed* upon the murderers of Hiram Abiff.

The allegation by the Rhode Island committee, that they considered it an unprofitable employment to be prying into Masonic secrets would be more plausible, if those secrets consisted only of the "signs, and tokens, and words, contrived to enable Masons, and none others, to enter lodges, and to distinguish one another from those not Masons;" but how is the fact? The tokens and pass-words are, to be sure, of the character described by Sir Tobey Belch in Shakspeare's Twelfth Night, "most excellent, sense-*less.*" But the *signs* are explanatory of the true meaning of the penalties, and when the committee compelled the Masons to give the *words* of their obligations, was it not an incongruous scruple of delicacy, to draw the veil over the coincident signs which give to those words their most energetic significancy?

Under the exceedingly accommodating indulgence of the investigating committee the Knights Templars of Rhode Island were permitted to skulk from all testimony relating to the fifth libation, denominated in Masonic language the *sealed obligation*. How the committee, consistently with their own rule, could release the witnesses from testifying to that *pious* solemnity, it is not easy to see. The *oath* of the Knight Templar has, like the rest, a penalty which is, having the swearer's skull smitten off and suspended to "rest high on spires," as the Masonic minstrels deliciously sing; and that oath and penalty the Rhode Island Knights did give according to contract with the committee. But the fifth libation is an obligation of higher order. The temporal penalties of cruel death and barbarous mutilation are not sufficient to bind the conscience of the Knight Templar. In the fifth libation he invokes eternal punishment upon his immortal soul. He calls upon God, his creator, to visit upon him at the judgment-day, not only his own sins, but all the sins of his fellow-mortal man, from whose skull he quaffs the cup of abomination and of mystery.

The most remarkable scene in the investigation of the Rhode Island committee was that in which William Wilkinson, a Knight Templar, and a man of most respectable character, was examined with reference to this sealed obligation—the fifth libation. The words always uttered before drinking the wine from the skull, were read to him from Allyn's Ritual, page 250, and he was asked whether they were administered to him on taking the Knight Templar's obligation. He answered, "These words made no part of the *obligation* which was administered to me on taking the Knight Templar's degree.

From this answer an unlearned and uninitiated person would naturally conclude that these words form no part of the ceremony of initiation to the Knights Templars' degree, and it is from denials of precisely the same character as this that the great mass of adhering Masons, ministers of the Holy gospel included, have labored to blast the credit of Allyn's and Bernard's books; but Mr. Wilkinson's denial hinged upon the word *obligation* only. There is, as I have remarked, another *obligation* administered to the Knight Templar, on taking his degree, and that obligation was among those furnished to the committee. That was the obligation which Mr. Wilkinson had in his mental contemplation when he denied that the words of the sealed obligation were part of *the* obligation administered to him. Had the examination rested there, well might the committee of the Grand Royal Arch Chapter of the United States have boasted of the *triumphant* acquittal of the Rhode Island Masons. But here the examination did not rest. Mr. Wilkinson was asked whether these said words were used in *any* ceremony of initiation to the Knights Templars' degree? His answer was, "In regard to the secrets or ceremonies of this or any other other degrees in Masonry, I neither affirm nor deny anything." Upon this there was some altercation between the witness and the chairman of the committee, who very justly considered this as an obligation which the Masons were bound to give; but instead of exercising the authority vested in the committee by the legislature, and exacting an answer, he argued with the witness to persuade him to answer, and finished by *submitting* to his refusal. This was indeed the triumph of Masonry; not the triumph of acquitted innocence, but the triumph of sturdy contumacy, setting at defiance the legislative authority of the state.

That Mr. Wilkinson should be ashamed to acknowledge that he had ever pronounced, with an appeal to God, such words as those, and accompanied them with such an action, is creditable to his sense of discrimination between right and wrong. The sealed obligation is not one of those signs, grips, tokens, or pass-words by which the Masonic fraternity discern the *genuine* from the *spurious* impostor. It is one of the obligations of the craft which the committee had determined to require, and which the Rhode Island Masons were bound by the terms of their agreement with the chairman of the committee to give. The fifth libation, therefore,—the potation from the skull of "Old Simon,"—and the invocation of all the sins, heinous and deadly as they may be, of another man upon the head of the self-devoted Knight Templar, are yet, so far as adhering Masonic acknowledgment is concerned, "undivulged crimes—unwhipped of justice." Mr. Wilkinson did not venture to deny that the words of the sealed obligation were precisely those recorded in Allyn's Ritual—he neither affirmed nor denied. The full adhering Masonic authentication of the sealed obligation is reserved for the investigation of a committee more resolute and less compromising with the transcendent sovereignty of Freemasonry than the Rhode Island Committee was found to be. A more searching investigation of the laws of the Masonic empire will be required to discover, in all its *loveliness*, that feature of its code. In the Rhode Island investigations another witness, a minister of the gospel, upon being asked if he had drank wine from a human skull, answered, "I do not know that it can affect the interest of any one whether I drank wine out of a skull, a tin-cup, or a basin." A third witness declined answering the question.

In the 251st page of Allyn's Ritual—the very next page after that which discloses the formula used in drinking the fifth libation—there is the following note:

"The sealed obligation is referred to by Templars, in confidential communications relative to matters of vast importance, when other Masonic obligations seem insufficient to secure secrecy, silence, and safety. Such, for instance, was the murder of William Morgan, which was communicated from one Templar to another under the pledge and upon this sealed obligation. The attentive ear receives the sound from the instructive tongue; and the mysteries of Freemasonry were safely lodged in the repository of faithful breasts —until it was communicated in St. John's Hall, New York, in an encampment of Knights Templars, March 10, 1828."

To this fact Mr. Allyn made oath before a magistrate in the city of New York, and that it was so communicated to him at an encampment of Knights Templars. Of the pains that have been taken to discredit Allyn's testimony it is not necessary for me to speak; but in the twenty-second of Col. Stone's Letters, page 238, there is a frank and full acknowledgment by him, himself a Knight Templar, that after having long totally disbelieved the statement, he did finally satisfy himself that it was substantially true.

With the thoughts that crowd upon me in re-

curring to this proof of the power and practices
of Masonry I will not now trouble you or the
public. The legislature of Rhode Island, after
such an investigation even as this, prohibited the
administration of all extrajudicial oaths. How
their committee could submit to the suppression of
Masonic testimony to the sealed obligation is not
easily explained. But the agonies of the Knights
Templars at the very call upon them to testify to
the sealed obligation are eloquent commentaries
upon the note in the 251st page of Allyn's Ritual,
and upon the candid acknowledgment in Col.
Stone's twenty-second letter.

And so, sir, the murder of William Morgan
was, by one of its perpetrators, regularly communicated to an encampment of Knights Templars
in the city of New York, in March, 1828, and
those Knights Templars (Col. Stone, who certifies
to the fact, knows not who they are—he thinks
them unworthy, but in the vocabulary of the
handmaid they are worthy Masons,) assisted this
murderer, and furnished him with the means of
escaping from the retribution of public justice
and the laws of the land!

And yet this was entirely conformable to the
laws of Masonry. It interfered in no respect with
the religion or politics of any one Knight Templar of the encampment! It was a memorable

exemplification of the promise to assist a worthy brother in extricating him from difficulty, whether he is right or wrong. It was most sincerely explanatory of the obligation to conceal the secrets of a worthy brother, murder and treason not excepted, or excepted at the option of the Sir Knight himself—and it did not even exact of the illustrious brotherhood that they should go barefoot to apprize this "western sufferer" of the danger with which he was threatened; and these transactions all occurred before the revelation of the obligations of the higher degrees of Masonry by the Le Roy convention of seceders, on the 4th of July, 1828. Of these facts, thus notorious, thus abominable, thus undeniable, why have the legislature, why has the executive of the State of New York, why have the grand-juries of the city never been informed! Why have the General Grand Encampment of the United States observed upon these acts of men under their jurisdiction a dignified silence? Why, but because they have resolved to adhere, and have recommended to the brotherhood under their jurisdiction to adhere, to the *ancient landmarks* of the institution.

Mr. Livingston, I shall here close the series of letters which I have addressed to you as the head and most conspicuous member of the Masonic fraternity in these United States—holding at the

same time offices of high dignity, power, and influence in the government of the Union. The
General Grand Royal Arch Chapter of the United
States, of which you are the grand high-priest,
did, at their triennial meeting at Baltimore last
November, highly commend certain chapters and
lodges which had changed, most essentially
changed, their own nature, by substituting the
study of the useful arts and sciences for the miserable fooleries of their pageantry, and did earnestly recommend to all the chapters under their
jurisdiction the same excellent reformation and
transformation. It was that recommendation
which suggested to me the idea of calling upon
you to accomplish a revolution still more useful
and commendable—the abolition of all the execrable oaths, obligations, and penalties, which, until
they shall be utterly abolished, are, and must be,
an indelible disgrace to the institution. If you
have power to convert your lodges into lyceums,
and your chapters and encampments into schools
of science, you can not lack the power of redeeming the institution from the infamy of lawless
oaths, of barbarous obligations, of brutal penalties.
With that infamy your institution is now polluted, as it is with the blood of William Morgan,
nor can the "labor" or "refreshment" of all the
Royal Arch chapters on the globe wash it out.

It is in your power, sir, to remove this stumbling-block and this foolishness from the institution over which you preside, forever. Look to the seventh chapter of the First Book of Kings and you will find that Hiram of Tyre, the widow's son, who worked at the building of the temple of Solomon, was not a Mason, but "cunning to work all works in brass." Whether this fitted him the better for the selection of the first contrivers of your order, as the founder of the craft, is a problem for your learned and especially for your clerical antiquarians to solve; but the fact that he was a workman in brass, and that the two pillars in the porch of the temple, Jachin and Boaz, were not works of Masonry, but of brass, stamps with gross imposture the whole history of the institution. In like manner every pretension of the order to historical connection with any portion of the Holy Scriptures is imposture, and must be known so to be to every intelligent minister of the gospel who takes upon himself your obligations.

The existence of such an order is a foul blot upon the morals of a community. The strength, the glory, the happiness of a nation, are all centered in the purity of its morals; and institutions founded upon imposture are the worst of all corruptions, for they poison the public morals at their fountains, and by multiplying the accomplices in guilt arm them with the confidence of virtue.

Whether your dignity as the head of the Royal Arch of this Union is to cease upon your departure from this country, or to continue during your absence, has not yet been announced to the world; but in either event be assured that neither your Masonic addresses, nor the proceedings of the General Grand Royal Arch Chapter of the United States, will henceforth pass without observation into oblivion.

JOHN QUINCY ADAMS.

TO MESSRS. TIMOTHY MERRILL, HENRY F. JANES, MARTIN FLINT, CHARLES DAVIS, EDWARD D. BARBER, SAMUEL N. SWEET, AND AMOS BLISS, COMMITTEE OF THE ANTI-MASONIC STATE CONVENTION, HELD AT MONTPELIER, IN THE STATE OF VERMONT, ON THE 26th OF JUNE, 1833.

QUINCY, 17 July, 1833.

Fellow-citizens:—I have received with great satisfaction your letter of the 27th ult., and with warm sensibility the resolutions which you have communicated to me of the Antimasonic Convention, held at Montpelier the preceding day.

The entire character of the institution of Freemasonry has not yet been displayed to the inspection of mankind. That it is essentially vicious and grossly irrational has been demonstrated beyond all possibility of reply; but the extent and degree to which it vitiates the morals and prostrates the intellect of its votaries has not yet been wholly disclosed. It is among the most ordinary symptoms of mental insanity that the faculty of reason is sound and vigorous upon every subject on which it is exercised save one, and at the same time irrecoverably distempered at that one. There are similar aberrations of *moral* principle in the conduct and character of individuals; and it has often been remarked that corporate bodies of men are capable of committing, without a blush, acts from which every individual of the association would shrink with instinctive horror.

The institution of Freemasonry is founded upon historical imposture,—and, can a Christian remark it without disgust?—upon imposture foisted upon sacred history; upon imposture falsifying the most awful truths of the gospel; upon imposture contaminating with unhallowed step the holy of holies itself.

The fable upon which the first three degrees of Masonry is founded carries absurdity and falsehood upon its face. There are fraud and duplic-

ity in the oaths and obligations into which the
candidates for initiation are unwarily drawn.
They are first made to invoke upon themselves
the penalties of death and brutal mutilation if
they should reveal the senseless secrets to be im-
parted to them; and then they are told a tale of
three Fellowcrafts, who, like them, had invoked
these penalties upon themselves, and upon whom
the *penalties had been executed*—not for revealing
the secrets which they had been sworn to keep,
but for murdering the first grand master in the
attempt to extort one of the secrets from him.
Ministers of the word of God have the oaths, in-
voking these penalties upon themselves, administered to them gratuitously, and take them for
nothing, while other poor, blind candidates are
laid under tribute for the privilege of burdening
their consciences with the same loads. After
taking them they are told that these have been
the standing penalties *for violation of the oaths of
secrecy* which they have taken, ever since *they
were executed upon the murderers of the first
grand master.* This first grand master of Masonry, they are told, was Hiram of Tyre, whom
the Holy Scriptures declare to have been a workman in brass; and they are assured that he was
murdered by three Tyrians, with Roman names,
three hundred years before Rome existed.

In this tortuous and fraudulent process of administering the oaths, and then delivering a lecture upon their pretended origin, some apology may be found for the hundreds of Masons in your state, and in others, who have so stoutly maintained in the face of their fellow-citizens that *they* never had taken any oaths incompatible with their duties to God and their country. To this process may be traced the utterly groundless *explanation* by which they have confounded treachery with martyrdom, and construed the penalty of death *for* revealing secrets into a sufferance of murder *rather* than reveal the secrets. The terms of the oaths are plain, explicit, and unequivocal. The promise is to suffer death as a penalty if the swearer reveals the secrets of Masonry or of Masons. And he is to suffer the death self-invoked, as the Tyrian Fellowcrafts, with Roman names, *did* suffer death for violation of Masonic law. The Tyro-Romans indeed had invoked these penalties upon themselves after committing murder as well as a breach of Masonic law; and Hiram, the brazier, grand master of Masons, had suffered death *rather* than reveal out of time and place the Master's word. Here is a confusion of ideas sufficiently indicative of fraud; and as the administration of the oaths is always oral, and the very writing or printing of them was

among the promises of the candidates never to do,
it is not surprising that thousands of Masons
should have taken them, not only without understanding what they were swearing to, but actually
believing that their promise was to die like Hiram, the victims of fidelity, and not, like his
murderers, to pay the penalties of treachery.

In the promises themselves, however, there is
nothing ambiguous or equivocal. They positively
contract the engagement to suffer the penalties of
death and bodily mutilation for any one violation
of the oaths which the candidate pronounces.
The death which a merciful man would not inflict
upon a dog, the Masonic candidate for *light* swears
he will suffer as a *penalty* if he should pronounce
the words Tubal-Cain, Shibboleth, or Mah-hah-
bone, out of time and place. Nay, if, like the
abbess of Andouillets and the nun in Tristram
Shandy, they presume to halve between them the
obnoxious words, to preserve the potency of the
spell, without infringing the laws of decorum—
not even the syllables Ja—and Chin, or Bo—and
Az, can be halved between two Masons, and publicly pronounced out of the lodge, but upon the
penalty of having both their throats cut across
from ear to ear. And this, and the like of this,
are the *ancient landmarks*, which the Grand Royal
Arch Chapter of the United States have earnestly

17

exhorted the chapters and lodges under their jurisdiction inflexibly to maintain.

Among the evidences of the true spirit and character of Freemasonry, which are daily disclosing themselves to the world, is this fanatical attachment and devotion to these ancient landmarks, which might be more properly denominated these incurable vices of the institution. To these vices how emphatically may be applied the remark of the moral poet, upon the propensity of human nature, to pass from detestation of vice first seen to the endurance and thence to the embrace of vice familiarized to the eye! If any one legislature of this Union should enact a law subjecting a citizen of these states, for the most atrocious crime that the heart of man could conceive or the arm of man could perpetrate, to any one of the Masonic penalties, one universal burst of indignation and abhorrence from the Atlantic to the Rocky Mountains would redeem the character of the American people from the disgrace inflicted upon it by such a legislative enactment. I hesitate not to declare the belief that not a jury could be assembled in this Union to convict, not a judge could be found to pass sentence upon, a man subjected to such a punishment by the sovereign legislatures of the land. And yet one of these penalties has been inflicted on a free citizen of this

Union—inflicted by the execution to the letter, of the secret, irresponsible, disavowed, and transcendental law of Freemasonry. It has been executed by Royal Arch Masons—executed by the hand of midnight and yet unpunished murder. The fact of this murder has been communicated by one of its perpetrators to an encampment of Knights Templars in the city of New York, and those Knights Templars, under the seal of the fifth libation, instead of delivering up the criminal to the lawful justice of their country, did, in strict conformity to their Masonic obligations, screen him from the punishment due to his crime, and furnish him with the means of escaping from that punishment forever.

It is, therefore, gentlemen, with unmingled satisfaction that I receive the assurance from you that the Antimasons of Vermont had determined to *persevere* in the righteous cause in which they have engaged, namely, that of breaking down the ancient landmarks of Freemasonry—landmarks which are the standing monuments of usurpation and crime. And whatever may be for years to come the fortunes of your cause, *perseverance* alone is the infallible pledge of your final success. We must not flatter ourselves that a moral evil so deeply rooted and of such gigantic dimensions can or will be eradicated in a short

time, or by intermitted exertions. We see the
Masonic institution, covered with all its enormi-
ties, upheld by clinging to both the great political
parties which divide the nation. We see the
Grand Royal Arch Chapter of the United States
taking into consideration the condition of Masonry
in the State of Vermont and pouring forth floods
of slander upon you and your associates, asserters
of the supremacy of the laws. But you and your
accusers are, in the presence of the American
people, alike amenable to the definitive tribunal
of public opinion. That opinion will ultimately
settle into a clear, simple, undeniable moral principle. The code of " Moloch homicide," embod-
ied in the laws of Freemasonry, will pass to its
appropriate region in Pandemonium, and one of
the sources of error and guilt prevailing in our
land will be exhausted and forever drained. For
my feeble contributions to effect this happy consummation, your approving voice is to me a precious reward. As a fellow-laborer with you for
the extinction of the brutal penalties of Freemasonry, my voice, so long as it has power to speak,
shall not be silent to an honest call; and when silenced, as it soon must be, by a summons to
another world, my testimony of abhorrence to
those penalties shall descend as an inheritance to
my children and to my country.

Accept, gentlemen, for yourselves, and for the convention whose resolutions you have communicated to me, the respect and the thanks of your friend and fellow-citizen.

JOHN QUINCY ADAMS.

TO JAMES MOOREHEAD, ESQ., SECRETARY OF THE MEADVILLE (PENN.) ANTIMASONIC CONVENTION.

WASHINGTON, 14 December, 1833.

Sir:—Your letter of the 30th of August last, communicating to me a copy of the resolution of thanks from the convention held at Meadville on the 28th of that month to my respected friend Mr. Rush and myself, for our services to the cause of pure morals against the institution of Freemasonry, was received at my residence in Massachusetts at a time when I was absent from it. Circumstances occurred, immediately after my return, inducing me to believe that there might be a propriety in deferring for some time the acknowledgment of the receipt of your letter, and the expression of my grateful sensibility to the approbation of the convention declared by their resolution, coupled as it was with a cheering exhortation to *perseverance* in the cause.

Believing that perseverance—unremitted, un-deviating perseverance,—is the only and the in-dispensable requisite for securing the final, the complete, and most desirable triumph of the cause of Antimasonry, I trust that so long as the fac-ulty of reason and the sense of justice shall be extended to me by the indulgence of my Maker I shall be found neither indifferent nor recreant to the cause. That cause I understand to be the abolition of the oaths, obligations, and penalties administered and taken for admission to the gen-eral degrees of Freemasonry,—obscurely indicated by the mandate of the General Grand Royal Arch Chapter of the United States, held at Baltimore in November, 1832, to the chapters and lodges under their jurisdiction,—indicated with an injunction of adherence to them, under the denomination of the *Ancient Landmarks of the Institution.*

The total demolition of these *ancient landmarks* I take to embrace the whole cause of Antimason-ry, and for the obvious reason that they are en-croachments upon the common rights and inva-sions of the common interests of the rest of man-kind; that they are impious, if not blasphemous invocations of the name of God; that they are fraudulent palterings with a double sense, saying one thing and intending another; that they are brutalities of thought and language shameful to be uttered by the lips of Christian men; and other objections to them of no trifling consideration to those who believe that the first inroads of corruption consist in familiarizing the mind to vicious thoughts, and the mouth to polluted words. But it is the common rights and common interests of mankind that are invaded by the *ancient landmarks* of Fremasonry; and it is the common interest of all that they should be, as public nuisances, *abated.*

And that they will be abated, depends upon perseverance alone. As sure as the daily revolution of the earth shall bring the source of light to ascend from the East, so surely shall perseverance sweep from the face of the earth, as common nuisances, the ancient landmarks of Freemasonry. Nor is it necessary, to this result, that what is commonly called political Antimasonry should be always or is even generally successful. Political Antimasonry is but one of the modes, though hitherto undoubtedly the most efficacious one, of combatting the Masonic institution. It is one of the exceptions to this mode of operation, that it necessarily manifests itself in the form of opposition to *persons,* and in the shape of punishment. It enlists, therefore, against itself not only the whole body of Masonic influence, but all the sympathies of friendship and all the weight of individual character and meritorious service. Its success then must and will be variable—fluctuating with the vicissitudes of transient popular opinion, and susceptible sometimes by its failure of retarding, as at others by success it may advance, the consummation devoutly to be wished. But I trust it may be considered by Antimasons as only *one* of their weapons against the common enemy—used with reluctance, and to be laid aside whenever Masonry herself shall be banished from the polls.

At the same time I fervently hope that the Antimasons of the free states of this Union will not be satisfied with the mere cessation of the meetings of lodges, chapters, and encampments, nor become indifferent to the cause, even when justice shall require of them to discard the question from the field of election. There is no question but that the Masonic oaths are all *unlawful.* But as in most of the states there is no specific penalty annexed to the administration of extrajudicial oaths, the law itself is outraged by it with impunity. In the states of Rhode Island and Vermont, statutes have recently been enacted annexing adequate penalties to the administration of extrajudicial oaths; so that in those states Masonry will no longer have the subterfuge to plead that her oaths are *not* unlawful, *because they are null and void.* If I am to credit the newspapers there has been a decision amounting to this, even by magistrates upon the bench in your State of Pennsylvania. Those magistrates, it is stated, were, all but one, themselves Masons; and if I understand the written opinion, reported as having been given by them, it was that without deciding whether the Masonic oaths were not lawful they held them to be voluntary promises, which could have no operation contrary to law, and therefore that a man who had taken those oaths was quite competent to be an impartial juror between Mason and Antimason. Now, although there is much *ingenuity* in this argument, and in the conclusion drawn from it, there is another conclusion to which it may lead other minds unilluminated with the floods of light which pour upon the pilgrim of the lodge-room. If there were specific penalties annexed to the administration of all extrajudicial oaths, Masonic judges would be relieved from all judicial non-committal, whether the Masonic oaths are lawful or not, and it would require one step further of Masonic *cooperation on the bench* to decide that a man bound by unlawful oaths, exclusively to favor one of the parties to a suit of law, is a very impartial juror between those parties, because the oaths he has taken, exclusively to favor one of them, *are unlawful.*

Sir, I wish the members of the convention who did me the honor to pass the resolution which you have communicated to me, to accept my thanks, and a hearty reciprocation with them of the Anti-masonic pass-word, "*Persevere*." It is the unconquerable spirit of all energetic virtue—the impregnable fortress founded upon the Rock of Ages.

I am, with great respect,

Your friend and fellow-citizen,

JOHN QUINCY ADAMS.

TO R. W. MIDDLETON, GETTYSBURG, PA.

QUINCY, 27 October, 1835

Dear Sir :—I have received your letter of the 19th instant, with the *Star* and *Republican Banner* of the same date. Amid the vicissitudes of alternate success and defeat, which in a very remarkable manner have attended the cause of political Antimasonry, I have witnessed with warm feelings of sympathy and admiration the *perseverance* with which it has been pursued in Pennsylvania, through good and evil fortune, to its signal triumph at this time, in the election of Mr. Ritner as governor of the commonwealth, and if I am to credit the public journals, of a decided majority of avowed Antimasons to the legislature.

Hitherto the Antimasons of Pennsylvania, though armed with a principle as pure as any that ever animated the heart of man,—though struggling against an institution foul with midnight murder, perpetrated in strict conformity to soul-ensnaring oaths and obligations, have yet been a feeble and persecuted minority,—persecuted for uttering the cry of indignation at a series of atrocious violations of the laws of God and man—persecuted for summoning the energies of virtue in the hearts of their fellow-citizens, to extinguish a secret and lawless conspiracy in the heart of the community against the equal rights of their fellow-men.

I trust the days of this persecution are past in Pennsylvania; that the government of that commonwealth, by the will of a decisive majority of its people, will be in the hands of Antimasons, and that by the wisdom and moderation of their measures they will redeem the state from the pollution of Masonic morals, and restore in triumph the supremacy of the laws.

I am, with great respect, dear sir,
Your obedient servant,
JOHN QUINCY ADAMS.

Address to the People of Massachusetts.

In the autumn of the year 1833 Mr. Adams was unanimously nominated at a large convention of members of the Antimasonic party, a candidate for the office of governor of Massachusetts. The call thus made upon him he did not feel at liberty to decline. The result was a triangular contest at the election, between the three political parties into which the people were divided, and the failure of a choice of governor by the requisite majority. According to the provisions of the constitution of Massachusetts the election then devolved upon the legislature about to meet in January, 1834. But no sooner was Mr. Adams made aware of the state of the popular vote, than he determined to decline to be further considered a candidate for the post. The reasons for his course, as well in accepting at first as in withdrawing afterward, he decided to submit in an address to the people of the commonwealth, which he caused to be published at the same time that he notified his decision in a letter directed to the speaker of the House of Representatives, at the opening of the session. The following is the address:

TO THE PEOPLE OF THE COMMONWEALTH OF MASSACHUSETTS.

Fellow-citizens:—For the first time within nearly half a century you have been so far unable to agree upon the person to whom the office of serving you in the capacity of your chief-magistrate should be committed for the ensuing year, that no one of the candidates presented by previous nominations to your favor has obtained a majority of your suffrages, and the case has occurred, in which, by the provisions of the constitution, your House of Representatives will be called to present to your Senate two of the four citizens, having the highest number of your votes, and of these two the Senate will be charged with selecting one as the governor of the state.

Of the four candidates having the highest number of votes my name stands the second; and supposing it from that circumstance probable that it might be one of the two offered by the House of Representatives for the choice of the Senate, I deemed it my duty to withdraw from the canvass, and to request the members of the House of Representatives to withhold their votes from me, with the assurance of my determination, founded on the sense of my own duties, not to accept the appointment should it be conferred upon me.

I have not thought it necessary or proper to assign to the legislature the reasons which have brought me to this determination. For the exercise of their functions it was only necessary that they should know the fact, and it would have been an unwarrantable consumption of *their* time, which is *your* property, to lay before them an exposition of motives, upon the correctness of which it would not be their province to decide, and which would neither require nor admit of any deliberative action appropriate to them.

This exposition of motives is, however, peculiarly due to that portion of my fellow-citizens who honored me by their nomination, and whose nomination I accepted. It is also due to you all— all having an interest in the issue of the election, and all being entitled to know; wherefore I have felt it justifiable to interpose between the provision of the constitution prescribed for the contingency which has occurred, and its absolute execution.

In accepting the nomination of the Antimasonic Convention at Boston, I was aware of the dissensions which agitated the commonwealth, and which I had witnessed with deep concern. I knew that the Antimasons as a party constituted a minority of the people of the commonwealth; that they were for the most part a detachment from that portion of the people who in recent times had been denominated National Republicans, and who under that denomination had embraced at least three fourths of the people of the state; that their views of general policy, both with regard to the administration of the general government and to that of the commonwealth, still coincided with those of that party; and I believed it an object of the highest importance to your welfare, and most especially with reference to your interest and influence in the affairs of the Union, that this breach should be repaired, and this discord restored to harmony. The Masonic controversy was the only point upon which the two divisions of the party were separated; but that separation I feared was irreconcilable. The party in opposition to the state government, and friendly to the present federal administration, was necessarily Masonic, by adherence to their chief, himself illustrious with Masonic acquirements and dignities. The National Republicans were Masonic, by the declared adherence of their chief to the same institution of which he was a distinguished member, and indications were not wanting that all the differences of principle between those two parties, ardent and bitter as they were, would be swallowed up in the transcendent common interest of Freemasonry. So it had emphatically proved in the State of Vermont, and such was, in my apprehension, likely to be the issue in Massachusetts. It was with extreme reluctance that I consented to be placed within the wind of this commotion, for I saw that it would bring me in collision with the party then still wielding the power of the state, and with whose general principles and policy my own were in full accord.

I had recently been re-elected, by the co-operation of that party, in the congressional district where I resided, to a seat in the House of Representatives of the United States. I had previously been nominated by a convention of the members of that party, as well as by an Antimasonic, and also a Republican convention, to represent the district of Plymouth in the last congress. At the expiration of that term of service I was again nominated by an Antimasonic, and also by a National Republican convention, to represent the district as newly constituted in the congress now assembled. Those nominations were both accompanied with resolutions approving, in the strongest and most gratifying terms, the manner in which I had executed the trust of representing Plymouth District; and although the district, as newly organized, was but partly the same with that which I had before represented, I was re-elected by a majority equally decisive with that of my previous election.

I had freely avowed my opinions of Masonry and Antimasonry, when the people of the district selected me to represent them in Congress. They were not the opinions of a majority of the people whom I was to represent, and they were sustained

18

by a very small though highly respectable minority of the people of the commonwealth. They were *unpopular* opinions, and therefore not the ground to be occupied by persons aspiring to popularity, or to its rewards.

The legislator of the most illustrious democracy of ancient times, Solon, made it a crime, punishable with death, for any citizen to shrink from taking his side upon any great political question which agitated and divided the people. Without approving the severity of this law, I consider the principle of its obligation as the vital spirit of republicanism. Republican government is essentially the government of public opinion, and it is good or bad government in proportion as public opinion is right or wrong. Public opinion is the aggregate of individual opinions, and the constitution, which secures to the citizen the right of *voting*, makes it his duty to form opinions by which the exercise of that right shall be governed. Every vote is an opinion manifested by free action, and whoever votes contrary to his opinion, or shrinks from the avowal of the opinion upon which he votes, is actuated by no republican spirit. In forming his political opinions every citizen must be governed by his own honest judgment, enlightened by consultation with others, and by such measures of information as he can obtain. But as this measure of information must necessarily be possessed by different persons in different degrees, the opinions of every individual must, in great multitudes of cases, be influenced by his confidence in others. To obtain the information necessary for forming a correct opinion upon political questions is a duty specially incumbent upon those who possess in any degree the *public* confidence; and having been one of those honored with the confidence of a large portion of my fellow-citizens, I have thought it my indispensable duty to make myself acquainted with the facts and the principles involved in the controversy relating to the Masonic institution.

The authentication of the facts, and the development of principles resulting from them, was necessarily slow and gradual. The struggle between the common rights of the people and the exclusive privileges of an oath-bound association, organized for extensive secretly concerted action, has been long protracted, and there is no present prospect of its termination. The kidnapping and murder of William Morgan, for merely avowing the intention to reveal the secrets of Freemasonry, was the first act which roused the attention of the people to the nature and character of this institution. In the transaction of that tragedy nine or ten of the most atrocious crimes that can be committed by men were perpetrated by deeds to which several hundreds of men were accessory; men not of the class of criminals instigated to guilt by poverty, ignorance, or ferocious individual passions, but men in the educated and influential conditions of life, many of them men in all their other relations to society of exemplary lives and conversation.

At the time of the murder of Morgan I was exercising the office of president of the United States. Neither the penalties of Freemasonry nor the practical execution of them, by the Masons who murdered him, were known to the public in general, nor to me. Freemasonry exercised an absolute control over all the public journals edited by members of the institution, and over many others by terror and intimidation. Months and years elapsed before the murder itself was fully proved—nor has it been judicially proved to this day. The names indeed of the men who took him from his dungeon on the 19th of September, 1826, and closed a torture of nine days' duration by sinking him in the middle of Niagara River, are perfectly well known. It is known that one of them was, according to Masonic law, upon avowal of his crime under the seal of the fifth libation, and under hot pursuit by the officers of justice, furnished, by an encampment of Knights

Templars in the city of New York, with the means of escaping from this country. But the witnesses to all these transactions are Freemasons, and, as accessories to the crimes of which they are cognizant, refuse or evade giving judicial testimony on the express ground that they might thereby criminate themselves. There are clouds of witnesses, but they are participators in the guilt; and thus it is that Masonry protects itself from the judicial authentication of its crimes by the very multitude of its accomplices, all bound by the invisible chains of secrecy.

But the trials of the Masonic outrages in the State of New York have exhibited other expositions of Masonic law. Masonic juries have been packed by Masonic sheriffs, for the express purpose not only of screening the guilty from punishment, but of falsifying the facts by presentments and verdicts known to themselves to be untrue. Masonic witnesses have refused to testify, and suffered imprisonment rather than disclose the facts known to them, even when they did not criminate themselves. Nor is this all. When conscience, bursting the bands of Masonry, has constrained Masonic witnesses to testify to crimes in which they themselves shared, and to the secrets of the craft, solitary Masonic jurors have refused their assent to verdicts, upon which all their fellows were agreed, on the avowed resolution that they would not believe any testimony of a seceding Mason.

The extent to which the public justice of the country had been baffled, and the morals of the people vitiated by Freemasonry, was therefore disclosed to me gradually, and by a slow process of time. Absorbed by other cares, and with time engrossed by the discharge of other duties, I was for years very imperfectly informed either of the laws of Masonry, or of the ascendancy they were maintaining over the laws of the land, or of the deep depravity with which they were cankering the morals of the people. Morgan's book was not published till some months after his death; and when published, the Masonic presses long labored in their double vocation of suppressing truth and propagating falsehood, by representing the disclosures of that book as false. Yet Morgan had revealed the secrets only of the first degrees, and the deepest of Masonic abominations were yet screened from the public eye. It was not until the fourth of July, 1828, that the convention of seceding Masons, held at Le Roy, made public the secrets, oaths, obligations, and penalties of the higher degrees. Nor were the proceedings of that convention made known to me till I found them in David Bernard's Light on Masonry.

To that book and its author permit me, my fellow-citizens, while recommending it to your perusal and meditation, to offer the tribute of unfeigned respect—a tribute the more richly deserved for the slanders which Masonic benevolence and charity have showered upon them. Elder David Bernard was a minister of the Genesee Baptist Association in the State of New York. He was a man of good repute, and of blameless life and conversation. Like many others, he was ensnared into the taking of fifteen degrees of Masonry, and was the intimate secretary of the Lodge of Perfection. He was one of the first seceders from the order, and from that time underwent every possible persecution from Masons, and the frequent danger of his life. Among the most interesting documents demonstrating the true spirit of Masonry, which have appeared in the course of this controversy, is the plain and unaffected narrative of the treatment which he received, and of the scenes which he witnessed at the meetings of lodges and chapters, *before* the murder of Morgan as well as after, from the time when it was projected in them. That it was so projected is established by his testimony, confirmatory of numerous other demonstrated facts.

To David Bernard, perhaps more than to any other man, the world is indebted for the revelation of the most execrable mysteries of Masonry, nor could he, as a minister of the word of God, have performed a service to his country and his fellow-christians more suitable to his sacred functions. It was principally by his exertions that the Le Roy convention of seceding Masons assembled and published the oaths, obligations, and penalties of the higher degrees of the order.

From the time of that publication the whole system of the Masonic laws and their practical operation, having relation to the disclosure of their secrets, have been gradually unfolding themselves, and the law and its execution have been continual commentaries upon each other. When the murder of Morgan was first perpetrated the instances were frequent of its being openly justified by members of the institution, as being but the execution of a *penalty* to which he himself had assented—as it certainly was. Another class of Masons, somewhat less resolute, contented themselves with maintaining that he was a perjured wretch for violating his oaths, and if he had been put to death, had only suffered what he deserved. A third class sturdily denied the facts even after everything but the last act of murder had been proved in regular judicial trials; and a fourth, intrenching themselves in ignorance, which they took care always to preserve by turning away their eyes from all evidence of the facts, rested their defense from the charge of Morgan's murder by professing *that they knew nothing about it.*

From the time when I first perused Elder Bernard's book, I became convinced that it was impossible for me to discharge my duties as a citizen to my country by knowing nothing about it. By a constant comparison of the laws of Masonry with their practical execution, from the robbery of Morgan's manuscripts and the abortive attempt to burn Miller's house, to the escape of Richard Howard from justice and from this country, a great multitude of facts combined to demonstrate the pervading efficacy of all the Masonic obligations. Measures always enfeebled and thwarted by Masonic influence were taken by the legislature and executive of the State of New York, to detect and bring the offenders to justice. The trials of the criminals were in progress; I endeavored to obtain information of their course and termination. The letters of Col. Stone upon Masonry and Antimasonry were addressed to me in consequence of inquiries made by me, to another person, and communicated to him. With regard to the facts ascertained by those trials, the reports made to the legislature of New York, and the proceedings of the first Antimasonic convention, held at Philadelphia, with the essays of William Slade upon the Masonic penalties, and the *defense* of Masonry by the grand lodge of Rhode Island, all concurred in furnishing a mass of information from which my conclusions were deduced.

I saw a code of Masonic legislation *adapted* to prostrate every principle of equal justice, and to corrupt every sentiment of virtuous feeling in the soul of him who bound his allegiance to it. I saw the practice of common honesty, the kindness of Christian benevolence, even the abstinence from atrocious crimes, limited exclusively by lawless oaths and barbarous penalties to the social relations between the brotherhood of the craft. I saw slander organized into a secret, wide-spread, and affiliated agency, fixing its invisible fangs into the hearts of its victims, sheltered by the darkness of the lodge-room and armed with the never-ceasing penalties of death. I saw self-invoked imprecations of throats cut from ear to ear, of heart and vitals torn out and cast forth to the wolves and vultures, of skulls smitten off and hung on spires. I saw wine drank from a human skull, with solemn invocation of all the sins of its owner upon the head of him who drinks from it; and I saw a wretched mortal man dooming himself to external punishment (when the last trump shall sound) as a guaranty for idle and ridiculous promises. Such are the laws of Masonry; such their indelible character—and with that character perfectly corresponded the history of the abduction and murder of Morgan, and the history of Masonic lodges, chapters, and encampments, from that day to the present.

To this general assertion numerous exceptions must be made, not only of individual Masons but of whole lodges and chapters,—I wish I could say of encampments, which have surrendered their Masonic charters, or silently dissolved themselves. Other lodges and chapters have ceased to hold their meetings, and I have heard of yet others, which, still holding their meetings, have ceased to administer any of the oaths. Besides these there are numbers of individual Masons who have silently seceded and withdrawn from that institution without renouncing it. It is probable that these exceptions include one third of all the Masons in the free states of this Union; and to them no observation of censure which I have made upon Masonry or upon Masons can apply. Their bearing is only upon adhering Masons and Masonry.

But of that censure the grand encampment, the grand chapter, and grand lodge of New York must take their full share. Their opinion of the

laws of Masonry, and of their true exposition, is
the same as mine. They have proved it by their
deeds. They knew that the kidnappers and
assassins of Morgan, the robbers of his manuscripts, the slanderers who falsely charged him
with larceny to seize upon his person and accomplish his destruction, the incendiaries of the house
of Miller; that the sheriffs who packed Masonic
juries, the juries who falsified their verdicts, the
witnesses who refused to testify, or deliberately
testified to falsehood; they knew that all these
had but acted in strict conformity and faithful
obedience to the letter and the spirit of the Masonic laws. So well did they know it, that far
from expelling any one of these criminals from
the fraternity they have hailed and recognized
them as worthy brothers of the craft, have cheered
them with consolation in their sufferings, indem-
nified them with money for their imprisonment,
and spirited away one at least of the ruffians,
whose hands were reeking with the blood of murder, from the public justice of their country.

All this, fellow-citizens, have I seen, through a
succession of time, now extending to more than
seven years. To inform myself of the facts I
deemed a duty of paramount obligation upon me,
as a man, a citizen, and a Christian; especially
after my release from the arduous duties of public

office. Had I been actuated by no other motives
than sympathy with the feelings of my own immediate neighborhood and friends, I trust they
would have needed no apology. It happened that
the attention of the inhabitants of my native
town of Quincy had been drawn to the facts of
the Morgan tragedy and of the laws of Masonry,
years before I came to reside among them. There
is a Masonic lodge in that town, and many of its
members are among the worthiest and most respected citizens of the place. Several of them
are my personal friends and kinsmen. When the
Masonic controversy first made its way into this
commonwealth the people of that town were
among the first who became acquainted with the
Masonic laws as they were divulged, and with the
Masonic crimes in New York, their natural progeny. A large majority of them became Antimasons, and so I found them upon my return among
them. The spirit of Antimasonry had already
pervaded the counties of Norfolk, Plymouth, and
Bristol; and the secession of the Rev. Moses
Thacher, and the controversies, ecclesiastical and
political, in which that step had involved him,
occasioned much agitation among this portion
of the people in the commonwealth.

In these dissensions I took no part; but I
should have been insensible to all my duties had

I closed my eyes to facts or turned my ear from argument, and smothered the sense of justice in my soul, for the privilege of blinking the public question which was convulsing the neighborhood in which I lived, by professing *to know nothing about it.*

Yet I did not intrude myself as a volunteer in the controversy. It had been erroneously stated in a newspaper, edited by a high Masonic dignitary in Boston, that I was a Mason. In answer to an inquiry from a person in New York, whether I was so, I had declared that *I was not, and never should be.* This letter, without my knowledge or consent, crept into the public prints; and from that day the *revenge* of Masonic *charity*, from Maine to Louisiana (I speak to the letter), marked me for its own. At the critical moment of the presidential election, in the counties of New York where Antimasonry was most prevailing, a handbill was profusely circulated, with a deposition upon oath, attested by a Masonic magistrate, of an individual, real or fictitious, swearing that he had been present at two different times (the dates of which were specified) with me at meetings of a masonic lodge at Pittsfield—a town in which I had never entered a house in my life.

This was the first punishment inflicted upon me by Masonic law, for declaring that I should never

be a Mason. The influence of Masonry upon that
presidential election was otherwise exerted with
considerable effect; and of the more recent election it decided, perhaps, the fate. I never noticed
either the false annunciation in the Boston *Sentinel* that I was a Mason, or the oath of the worthy
brother of the square and compass that he had
twice met me at the lodge in Pittsfield. They
were both calumnies, as strictly conformable to
Masonic laws as to Masonic benevolence, and
have been followed up by slanders coined at the
same mint and circulated through all the frater-
nizing presses of the land.

I have stated to you, fellow-citizens, the reasons
and motives which have actuated me in the part
I have taken in the Masonic and Antimasonic
controversy. To obtain an accurate knowledge of
the facts, and of the *real* laws of Freemasonry,
and to bring them to the test of pure moral principles, I believed to be my indispensable duty; and
having done that, it was no less my duty to bear
my testimony on every suitable occasion both to
facts and principles.

Col. Stone's letters contained an exposition of
Masonic law, from a Knight Templar who had
withdrawn but not seceded from the order; an
exposition as favorable as the hand of a friend
could make it, consistently with the candor of

truth.   It was palliative, excusatory, apologetical, for Masonry in its fairest colors; and it first put forth the avowal that the Masonic obligations were *not* among the secrets of Masonry.   This was a point upon which the most eminent dignitaries of the craft differed among themselves; but in the meantime the obligations were *kept* secret. They never had been divulged till the publication of Morgan's book since forgotten revelations of Jachin and Boaz, the author of which is understood to have suffered the same fate as Morgan.

Col. Stone gave the original oath, obligation, and penalty, the only one taken at and long after the primitive institution of the order.   He also referred in his book to a manuscript of the oaths, obligations, and penalties of the first seven degrees, including the Royal Arch, as they have generally been administered in the lodges and chapters of New England; and he afterward, at my request, transmitted to me the manuscript, which is now in my possession.   It is a complete, though abridged, summary of Masonic law to the degree of Royal Arch; and the volume of Col. Stone gives the fair and full history of the execution of that law, in its conflict of five years with the sovereign authority of the State of New York.

In those letters Col. Stone had also referred to an opinion, previously expressed by me to him in conversation, that the first step in Freemasonry, the initiatory rite, the Entered Apprentice's oath, was vicious, immoral, and unlawful. By this publication of my opinion, which I had not authorized, but to which I could have no objection, I felt myself called upon to expose, by a strict analysis of the Entered Apprentice's oath, the reasons upon which I had passed that summary sentence of condemnation upon it. I addressed therefore to Col. Stone, for publication in the paper of which he is a joint editor in New York, the four letters on the Entered Apprentice's oath, which have since been extensively circulated, but which, such is the power of Masonry over the periodical press, it required no small exertion of fortitude and intrepidity in him to publish.

I shortly afterward received from Benjamin Cowell, a citizen of Rhode Island, a letter, asking my opinion in what manner this vicious and immoral institution could most effectively be put down. In my answer to him I suggested two obvious modes of effecting that object. The one, that the Masons themselves should abolish or cease to administer the oaths, obligations, and penalties; and the other, that the administration of them should be prohibited under adequate penalties by legislative enactment in the several states.

That they should be voluntarily abandoned by

19

the Masons themselves was my first wish, because that would have been a meritorious act—an act now sanctioned by the example of the lodge of my own constituents at Plymouth, to the members of which I tender hereby my warmest thanks, and which, if followed by all the lodges, will, I have no doubt, (as it should,) put down all political Antimasonry within the commonwealth forever. But the General Grand Royal Arch Chapter of the United States, at a meeting held at Baltimore, had just issued an edict forbidding this voluntary consummation; and there were numerous other indications, that however multitudes of individual Masons, lodges, and chapters were disposed to yield to the voice of reason, of religion, and of law, and to cease from the further administration of their hideous vows, this was not the temper or intention of the high and leading members of the institution; and it was apparent that the principle of subordination, so essentially woven into the texture of the order, would deter most of the inferior and affiliated associations of the fraternity from breaking their fetters and dissolving their bands. I believed, therefore, that the aid of legislative prohibition with penalties would be indispensable for abating this moral nuisance in the community; and I recommended that the administration of the Masonic oaths should be prohibited by law, upon penalties of fine and imprisonment, adequate to *deter* from the administration of them in *future*.

I take this occasion, fellow-citizens, to justify myself before you from an aspersion which the committee of the convention of National Republicans at Worcester (who resolved that their party *must* be a majority of the people, not only of the commonwealth but of the Union,) did not disdain, in their zeal, to make that majority cast upon me in their address to you. The committee assured you that Antimasonry was not a proper ground for political controversy, and as it did not suit their purposes fairly to state to you the real question between Masonry and Antimasonry, they presented you a fictitious one, invented in the lodge-room, and adopted by them as their own. They told you that Antimasonry was a persecuting spirit, the object of which was to deprive Freemasons of their rights; and by quoting with inverted commas a passage of my letter to Mr. Cowell, they perverted it into an assertion that I had recommended a law to punish men with "fine and imprisonment" for being Masons. I recommended no such thing; but as I know that some of the members of the committee who signed that address have learned to read, and as some of them may peradventure in times past have professed to be my friends, I take the liberty of a friend in recommending to them the next time they shall be charged with addressing you, in behalf of a party which *must* have a majority, to respect *you* if they will not respect themselves; to respect you by abstaining from the slander of a political adversary, not less by a palpable misrepresentation than by willful falsehood.

I have great satisfaction in observing that within two months after the publication of the extracts of my letter to Mr. Cowell, the legislature of Rhode Island did, with great unanimity, enact a law prohibiting the administration of extrajudicial oaths, upon penalties of fine and political disfranchisement, which last is rather more severe, but more appropriate to the offense, than that which I had proposed. It is to be presumed that while that law remains in force the General Grand Royal Arch Chapter of the United States, which is to meet again at the city of Washington in December, 1835, will not again enjoin upon the chapters and lodges under their jurisdiction, at least within the State of *Rhode Island*, a rigid adherence to the *ancient landmarks* of the order,—that is, to these very extrajudical oaths. They will, I trust, abstain also from repeating the same injunction to the chapters and lodges in the State of Vermont, where a similar law, prohibiting in substance the administration of the Masonic oaths, has lately been enacted. It happens that these same two states of Rhode Island and Vermont are the identical states in which the report of the committee of the General Grand Royal Arch Chapter of the United States affirmed that Masonry had triumphantly sustained itself, and with regard to Rhode Island that it had been *sustained by the legislature.*

Fellow-citizens, I indulge the hope that before the next meeting of the General Grand Royal Arch Chapter of the United States *your* statute-book will present for their consideration the same disposal of the "ancient landmarks" of Freemasonry; for when *you* shall have set *your* seal of reprobation upon those abominable appeals to the name of God, these atrocious obligations, those butchering and blasphemous penalties, and when the Freemasons of your commonwealth shall *submit* to your will, in this enactment, Antimasonry within *your* borders will be extinct—mine at least will "die away." There is not a Freemason in the state to whom I bear personally a particle of ill-will. There are many for whom I entertain a warm and cordial friendship, even of those who have declared to you that Freemasonry *knows* no penalty beyond admonition, suspension, and expulsion. I am willing to believe that they did not understand, so well as the murderers of Morgan, the oaths they had taken. Even of those who have been slandering me without measure and without stint, I am ready to allow that they are only fulfilling their Masonic obligations, and following their vocation, and that they have the example of *my friends* of the National Republican Worcester convention committee, to sustain them. Whatever of evil there is in Antimasonry is but an aggravation of the sins of Masonry herself.

I am aware of the objections to what is called political Antimasonry, which have hitherto deterred a large majority of you from resorting to it as an extinguisher to the baleful light of Freemasonry. One of the most fascinating allurements of the "handmaid" has been her influence in promoting the political advancement of the brethren of the craft. Silent and secret in her operations, she raised them with invisible hand to place and power, and one of the first discoveries made by Antimasonry was that three fourths of all the offices within range of the cable-tow were occupied by Masons. This had become in fact the great and absorbing employment of lodge, chapter, encampment, and consistory; not while the tyler with drawn sword was at the door; not while the master, grand master, high-priest, or

illustrious sir knight was reading lessons of
benevolence and charity, from the pages of Holy
Writ; not while the slipshod, hoodwinked, halter-
ed, poor, blind pilgrim was perambulating the lodge
with pointed dagger at his breast, in search of
light; not even in the passage from labor to refreshment, nor in the choruses of Masonic minstrelsy,
so congenial to that *decent* mimicry of the ineffable Jehovah in the burning bush. All these
were but the types and shadows of what was to
come; all this was but the outward shell to the
kernel of Masonic brotherhood. The principle
of preference established by the Masonic code of
politics was that a brother of the craft was to
be preferred to any other of *equal* qualifications.
It was the *odd trick* of the game, and it shuf-
fled all the *honors* into the hands of the Masonic
partner.

This statute of Masonic law was in the year
1816 promulgated under the seal of the compass
and square, by a Master Mason in the Boston
Sentinel, the same paper which afterward so *vo-
raciously* declared me to be a member of the
order. Little attention was paid to this political
pass-word at the time. It was taken for a mere
common electioneering paragraph. Its operation
was neither seen nor suspected. The obligation
had not then been sharpened into a positive

promise upon oath, clinched as usual with the penalty of death, but as a general portion of the law of exclusive favor to the brethren of the craft, operating unseen, and visible even in its effects only to the initiated; it was, as it always must be, a conspiracy of the few against the equal rights of the many; anti-republican in its sap, from the fruit blushing at the summit of the plant to the deepest fiber of its root.

It was, perhaps, this monopoly of public office, by the Masonic guide to the ballot-box, which first suggested to the Antimasonic party the expedient of counteracting its effects by adopting the same principle and reversing its application. It needed nothing more. If the Mason was bound, between candidates of equal qualifications, to prefer the brother of the craft, the Antimason was but turning upon him his own tables, in giving the same preference to the brother Antimason. Yet this is the principle openly avowed as a fundamental law of the Masonic fraternity, but which turned upon themselves raises a universal outcry of proscription, disfranchisement, and persecution.

Fellow-citizens, there is in my mind an objection to the principle itself. It is but a modification of the selfish, intolerant, and exclusive principle of party spirit. In the Masonic code and practice it has the additional vice of *secret* operation.

When Antimasonry first raised its head in New
York it found three fourths of all the *elective* offices in the state in the hands of *Masons.* The
proportion of Masons to the whole population
was not one fiftieth part. How is it with you
now? Look to the delegation from your city in
your House of Representatives. Boston, to speak
in round numbers, has ten thousand citizens qualified by your constitution and laws to serve as
representatives in the general council. Of these ten
thousand, one thousand may be Masons. Boston
had last year sixty-three members in the House.
Of these, by relative proportion of numbers, there
should have been six, or at most seven Masons.
How many were there? Nearly thirty. Of the
number this year elected, the Masonic proportion
is not less. Here are then nine thousand citizens
of Boston, qualified to serve as representatives in
the legislature, virtually disfranchised, that is, deprived of the enjoyment of their rights by the
preference of brother Masons over others of equal
qualifications, and the exclusive selection of Masons to fill the seats, the access to which ought,
by your constitution and laws, to be enjoyed
equally by all.

Look to the delegation in your Senate from the
county of Worcester, the very throne of Masonry
in the commonwealth. There are in that county

say ten thousand citizens eligible to the Senate.
One tenth of that number may be Masons—one
member in the Senate would be more than their
fair proportion of the representation. They have
five out of six. Now if the Freemasons of Worcester county were, like the patricians of ancient
Rome in her early days, an order of nobility, *exclusively* eligible to seats in the Senate, what would
be the difference of the result from that which is
here effected by the Masonic preference of a
brother of the craft over others of equal qualifications?

I shall not now inquire what influence this combined action of Masonic agency, by the united nu-
meric power of the city of Boston and the county
of Worcester in your legislative councils, has, and
must have over the administration and policy of
the whole commonwealth. Its power will be
pre-eminently conspicuous in the proceedings of
your legislature. I only invite your attentive observation of its effects. Watch the movements of
your general court, especially upon every subject
connected with the supremacy of Masonry, and
observe the issues, as they may affect your own
interests, of the Masonic sympathies between the
delegations from the city of Boston and the county
of Worcester.

The preference at elections, of Antimasons for

candidates of their own opinions, is nothing more
than the application of the Masonic rule and practice of electioneering to themselves. It is only
justifiable as a defensive measure, and as a means
of counteracting the rapacious grasp of Masonry
at all the offices of the land.

In my letter to Mr. Cowell, I did not express
my approbation of political Antimasonry even to
the whole of this extent. I confined my approbation to the election of members to the state
legislature, and to them only until statutes prohibiting with adequate penalties the administration of Masonic oaths should be enacted. The
legislatures of Rhode Island and Vermont *have*
enacted such statutes; and if the Masons in those
two states *submit* to them, Masonry within them
must ultimately die, as corporations are extinguished, by the death of all their members.

A far manlier and more honorable course would
be that proposed by Samuel Elliot, a Royal Arch
Mason of Vermont, a stranger to me, but a man
who deserves well of his country, who had the
intrepidity to call upon his brethren and companions of the order to yield to the unequivocal voice
and wishes of their fellow-citizens; to lay down
their childish pageants and preposterous dignities; to cast away their paper crowns and lackered
scepters; their globe and cross-crowned miters,

and their harlequin wooden swords of knight-hood; and to emerge from the tawdy honors of grand kings, and high-priests, and princes of the royal secret, and resume the plain, unembroidered, laceless, but comfortable and decent garb of re-publican citizens. This proposition was indeed perilous to him who made it, and the flood-gates of slander, according to the ancient usages of the order, were immediately opened upon him. But it was regularly considered and debated at a meet-ing of the grand lodge of Vermont, at which were present one hundred and twenty members delegated from the several secular lodges in the state. Of these, forty-one voted for accepting the proposal of Mr. Elliot, one third of the whole number; and it was before the act of the legisla-ture prohibiting the administration of extrajudi-cial oaths. Let the moral Antimasons who con-cur in the opinion that the Masonic oaths and obligations are vicious and immoral, but who are unwilling to manifest this opinion at the ballot-box, reflect upon this fact. Immediately before it occurred the two great political parties had com-bined together, and burying all their distinctive principles, and distributing prospectively between them all the offices and honors of the state, had united in one great and convulsive effort to put down Antimasonry. It failed. The atmosphere of the Green Mountains diffuses around them not only a physical but moral and political air too pure for the contamination of political prostitution. The people at the ballot-boxes bastardized the fruits of this unnatural union, and prostrated both the parties to it before the lofty spirit of Antimasonry.

The immediate consequence of this event was the convocation of the grand lodge of the state to consider the proposition of the Royal Arch companion Elliot; and although it did not then succeed entirely, one important step to the dissolution of the order was taken. The grand lodge did grant a permission to the secular lodges under their jurisdiction to dissolve themselves—a process which it is earnestly to be hoped they will generally pursue; for let the institution but be once formally extinguished by the voluntary act of its members in one state of this Union, and I harbor not a doubt that it will very shortly vanish from the land.

It is to this voluntary relinquishment of the whole system of Freemasonry by its own members that I look for that great moral and political reform which will be effected by the extinction of the order. To this sacrifice of their prejudices and their pride, of their vanities and their follies, they must be brought by the power of permanent

and quickening public opinion. I have approved
of the ballot-box as *one* of the modes of manifest-
ing this opinion; and this the more readily because it was at the ballot-box that the maleficent
power of the Masonic trowel was cementing the
edificé of the polluted temple. But I have not
deemed the ballot-box the only, or even the favorite, weapon of Antimasonry. I have sanctioned
the partial resort to it with reluctance, and would
rejoice to see the day when it should be no
longer necessary. I have indeed never resorted
to it myself, by interfering in any election against
a Masonic candidate, and have in the discharge
of my own duties preferred other modes of operating, to the extent of my poor ability, upon public opinion.

It was this last motive that induced me to publish the four letters to Col. Stone, upon the Entered Apprentice's oath, in which, by a minute
analysis of it in all its parts, the appeal to God,
the promise and the penalty, it was my purpose to
prove it *wrong*, vicious, unlawful, and immoral—
contrary to the principles of Christianity, of humanity, of law, of eternal truth and justice. To
those letters, now fifteen months published, not
one word of reply has ever appeared.

When the General Grand Royal Arch Chapter
of the United States, at their last triennial meet-

ing, issued their mandate and exhortation to the
chapters under their jurisdiction, and their subordinate lodges, to turn themselves into lyceums
and schools of useful knowledge, but adhere to
their *ancient landmarks*,—meaning their oaths, obligations, and penalties,—I saw in their proceedings a new occasion for an appeal to the moral
sense of the community. *Edward Livingston*, then
secretary of state of the United States, was re-elected their grand high-priest, an office which he had
occupied for the three preceding years. The personal relations between this gentleman and myself
had uniformly been of a friendly character. As
the legislator of a criminal code for Louisiana,
and as on more than one occasion a sound expos-
itor of the principles of our national constitution, he had acquired my esteem, my admiration,
I had almost said my veneration. In his code for
Louisiana he had proposed the total abolition of
the punishment of death, and in his report to the
legislature had supported this proposition with a
power of reasoning and of eloquence which,
without entirely convincing my judgment, had
been viewed by me as at once the proof of a vig
orous mind and the pledge of a benevolent heart.
It appeared to me impossible that such a man
could read the letters on the Entered Apprentice's
oath without either assenting to their argument

or perceiving the indispensable necessity to the
institution of refuting it. I could not believe it
possible that *he* should deliberately consider the
oaths, obligations, and penalties, which it was yet
his official duty to administer, either innocent, or
harmless deceptions—speaking, in the name of
God, one thing and meaning another. As the
general grand high-priest of Masonry in the
United States, he was bound to be the official de-
fender of the institution against any serious
charge of unlawfulness or immorality, and he
had, perhaps inconsiderately, assumed not only
that character, but that of an accuser of Antimasonry at the bar of public opinion, in his inaugural address at his first installation. I sent him,
therefore, a copy of the letters on the Entered
Apprentice's oath, and addressed six letters to
himself, calling upon him to defend his institution
or to purge it of its impurities; to maintain his
charges against a numerous and respectable class
of his fellow-citizens, or to retract them.

There are men upon whom the consciousness of
having done great wrong to others produces little remorse, unless awakened to the sense of their
own injustice by feeling the application of the
scourge from another hand. I did not believe
Mr. Livingston to be a person of such a character.
I gave him credit for honest and generous feeling.

I believed that if reminded of a gross injury committed inadvertently by himself in the form of erroneous imputations upon others, he would hasten to repair it. The voluntary reparation of its own injustice is one of the most glorious features of true magnanimity. Mr. Livingston did not notice my letters—not even by acknowledging the receipt of them. Had they been upon any other subject, I have reason to know that they would have been received with friendly acknowledgment and courtesy. But you will recollect that in his inaugural address upon his installation as the grand high-priest of the General Grand Royal Arch Chapter of the United States, to his brethren and companions, he advised them that if the *cause* and the *effect*,—if the oaths, obligations, and penalties of Masonry as the *cause*, and the literal execution of them upon Morgan and Miller as the *effect*,—followed by the baffling of the sovereign authority of the State of New York in all its exertions to bring the murderers and incendiaries to justice; if the throat-cutting, emboweling, heart and vital tearing, skull-smiting, hanging, drowning, quartering, double and treble eternal damnation of the penalties on one side, and if on the other the apathy of the Masonic executive government of New York, the packing of Masonic juries by Masonic sheriffs, the perjuries and pre-

20

varications of Masonic witnesses, the grants of
Masonic funds by the grand lodge and grand
chapter of New York to the convicted and con-
fessing kidnappers of Morgan, under the denomination of western sufferers; if the illustrious and
successful achievement of the encampment of
Knights Templars in New York, in rescuing from
the gibbet and conveying beyond the seas one
of the murderers of Morgan;—if all this should
be pressed home and hard upon the fraternity,
they should meet it all with *dignified silence*.

I could not be surprised, therefore, at finding
him practice upon his own precept, or at discovering the difference of *moral principle* between
Edward Livingston the legislator of Louisiana
and Edward Livingston the general grand high-
priest of the Royal Arch Masonry of the Union.

You will observe, fellow-citizens, that neither
in my letters to Col. Stone nor those to Edward
Livingston was there one word of political Antimasonry. The object of the letters to Col. Stone
was to prove by plain and unanswerable argument that the Masonic institution in its first rite
of initiation is radically and incurably vicious.
That of the letters to Mr. Livingston was to prevail
upon him to exercise his great and powerful influence to discard those oaths, obligations, and
penalties, which are the indelible disgrace of the

order. To these letters no answer has been made or attempted.

When my letter to Mr. Cowell was first published it was in like manner left unnoticed. But when the recent election came on, then came the season for revenge; then it was that a part of my letter to Mr. Cowell was produced, published, and trumpeted abroad, and by the same process which in Masonic logic and language expounds a throat cut across from ear to ear to mean *expulsion* from a lodge,—a declaration that I would, if a member of a state legislature, vote for the enactment of a statute prohibiting upon pain of fine and imprisonment the administration *in future* of the Masonic oaths,—was represented as a recommendation to cast into prison every Freemason to whom the oaths have been administered heretofore. And this Royal Arch *mistake* the committee of the Worcester convention did not disdain, in addressing *you*, to adopt and make their own.

Before entering upon the field of the Masonic controversy I had not only deemed it my indispensable duty to possess myself of the facts and principles material to it, but to contemplate the consequences which would, and those which might, result from being involved in it myself. In the district which I was then to represent in congress, about two fifths of the population were

Antimasons; but the political majorities in both the counties of Plymouth and of Norfolk were Masonic, or at least adverse to Antimasonry. Throughout the commonwealth the Antimasons were in numbers scarcely one fifth, and in Boston not more than one tenth, of the voting citizens, while the combined concentrated action of the three Masonic strongholds of the state—Boston, Worcester, and Salem,—had already succeeded, in accordance with the mandate of the general grand high-priest of the Royal Arch Chapter of the United States, in raising clouds of obloquy and persecution against the cause of Antimasonry itself, and against all who espoused it. I saw very distinctly that Antimasonry was not the path of ambition. It was certain to give umbrage to a large majority of the people of the state under their *then* existing impressions. It would probably displease three fifths of my own constituents, whose displeasure might soon be manifested at the ballot-box. Their suffrages had not been solicited by me, nor had I the most distant imagination that I should ever appear as a candidate for the suffrages of the people of the state, as their chief magistrate. I had at other periods of my life enjoyed large portions of their favor, and had received recent proof that that favor was not abated. I had nothing more ever to ask of them but their good opinion, and that was inexpressibly precious to me. Why should I expose myself to the risk of forfeiting it altogether, without any earthly object or prospect of benefit to myself?

My only answer to this question is, It was the cause of truth and pure morals; it was an abused and calumniated cause; it was a cause deeply interesting to my constituents, to my fellow-citizens, and to my country.

My re-election to congress by an undiminished majority of my constituents had been very gratifying to me, as a token that the portion of my fellow-citizens in that district, opposed to Antimasonry, were so far disposed to tolerate my disagreement in opinion with them upon this point that they did not consider it as a reason for withdrawing their confidence from me.

The Masonic denunciation and misrepresentation of my letter to Mr. Cowell had been tried against me there, without effect. Neither Masonry nor Antimasonry were subjects of controversy in congress, and it was enough for me know that the great mass of my constituents were satisfied that my zeal for Antimasonry had in no wise interfered with the faithful discharge of my duties as their representative.

The Antimasonic convention held at Boston in

September were pleased to nominate me as their candidate for your suffrages as chief magistrate of the commonwealth for the ensuing year. I knew that their chief object in tendering to me the nomination was to make an effort to restore the harmony between the two divisions of the National Republican party, which had long constituted the vast majority of the people of the commonwealth. They were as yet separated only by that line. I believe there was no neutral ground. Aware of personal prejudices against me, existing in a respectable portion of the National Republican party, upon other and long-standing collisions between them and me,—and the public service in which I was engaged being more adapted to the experience of my past life, and better suited to considerations of interest to me, though of none to the public,—I had very sincerely hoped and expected that the views of the Antimasonic party would unite upon some other citizen as their candidate for the chief magistracy of the state. Their nomination was however placed upon grounds which it was impossible for me to withstand; and as I knew it was on their part a tender of the olive-branch to those of their fellow-citizens with whom they had long walked in the strength of united councils, and from whom they had parted only at the dictate of a pure, uncompromising, *moral* principle, I accepted their nomination in the same spirit in which it was tendered, and in my answer of acceptance expressed to them my determination, if the suffrages of the people should confirm their nomination, to carry into effect, to the utmost extent of my ability, *their* purpose of restoring harmony to the commonwealth, and of promoting, as far as possible, that of the Union.

But in this acceptance, you will perceive, fellow-citizens, there was a condition expressed,—and there was also one implied. The expressed condition was, the contingency that the suffrages of the people should confirm the nomination. I was resolved in no event to hold the office of governor of the commonwealth from any hands other than those of a majority of the people themselves, for the obvious reason that it was impossible for the representative of a minority of the people to be the suitable agent for promoting harmony among them. If, therefore, a majority of the people should reject the nomination accepted by me, it was clear that the restoration of harmony, if to be effected at all, must be accomplished under happier auspices than my elevation to your highest trust. A failure, therefore, of a single vote short of a majority, constituting me your governer by your own voice,

would have been a decisive indication to me that
harmony could only be promoted by me, not
by persevering in the contest of an election, but
(if in any possible manner) by retiring from it.

The implied condition was dependent upon the
same contingency. It was that my election should
involve no dereliction of other public duties with
which I was charged. I was a representative elect
of the twelfth district of the commonwealth in the
congress of the United States. Of the importance
to your interests and to the welfare of the Union
that you should have a full representation in the
popular branch of the national legislature, at all
times and without intermission, I had always had
a strong impression, and have now an impression
much deepened by the painful experience of the
last congress, in which, for the want of that full
representation, you suffered in various ways gross
injustice, and particularly by the curtailment of
your constitutional right in that representation
itself. As the representative of the twelfth district, I held it to be my duty to enter into no engagement which should deprive my constituents
of their voice in the national legislature for a
single day. ⌊If, therefore, even before your annual
election was held, I had seen reason to *expect* that
I should be chosen your governor by the majority
of the people, I should have resigned my seat in

congress in ample time to give my constituents the opportunity before the meeting of congress to elect another representative in my place. The convention held at Worcester the first week in October rendered this measure on my part unnecessary, and in resolving to take my seat in congress I assumed the fulfillment of duties incompatible with my acceptance of the office of governor of the commonwealth.

In saying this, fellow-citizens, I intend no reflection upon the candidate of the National Republican party for your suffrages as governor; nor do I mean to say or insinuate that he is or should be bound by the principles of conduct which my sense of duty prescribes to me for the government of mine. He was nominated by a convention, who, instead of tendering or accepting an olive-branch, resolved that they *must* have a majority, and set all other parties in the commonwealth at defiance. He had no call from them to promote harmony; and if in the event of his election he should, as I hope and trust he will, do so, it will be in the indulgence of his own fair and honorable spirit, and not by following the impulse of that convention, who, representing the remnant of a party which once had a majority, seem to have persuaded themselves that it must necessarily last forever.

He has besides this a vote of the people by
several thousands larger than mine; and although
by the provisions of your constitution this is not
sufficient for his election, nor even to control the
choice of your representatives in the legislature,
it is yet amply sufficient reason for me to withdraw from a contest with him, but not calling upon him to withdraw from a contest with me, or
with either of the other candidates nominated by
the convention.

He is also the representative of one of your districts in the congress of the United States, and
his acceptance of the office of governor will necessarily vacate his seat, and leave his constituents
for a time (I hope a very short one) unrepresented.

Mr. Davis does not estimate the evil and danger of incomplete representation in the congress
of the United States as of so great magnitude as
I do; and I regret to say that your opinions upon
this subject appear to correspond more with his
sentiments than with mine. There is a great
defect in your laws, relating to the election of
members of the House of Representatives of the
United States. They require an absolute majority
of all the votes returned, and make no provision
for the contingency frequently occurring when
such majority can not be obtained. This is one of
the cases in which practicable good is sacrificed to

theoretic perfection; a principle unsound in morals and mischievous in politics. The consequence of it is, that by adhering to it inflexibly you voluntarily deprive yourselves of the full representation to which you are entitled.

At the commencement of the last congress two of your districts were thus unrepresented, and the immediate consequence of that was the choice of a speaker assuredly not favorable to *your* interests. Had those two vacancies been filled, another person, less hostile to you, would have been chosen. Committees would have been appointed with more regard to impartiality, and you would not have been deprived by political management of one thirteenth part of your right in the representation, as you have been, for the next ten years. Nor is this the only or the greatest wrong you are suffering and will suffer by your perseverance in stripping yourselves of your own right. At the time to which I allude your whole delegation in the House, with the exception of Mr. Davis, were so impressed with the importance of this defect in your laws that they addressed a joint letter to Governor Lincoln, requesting him to recommend a revision of them to the legislature. He did so; but no effectual remedy was provided. You remained for nearly the whole congress unrepresented for one of your districts; for nearly

the whole of a long and most important session
unrepresented for both; and now, at this day,
shorn of your constitutional right to one member
by a grossly unjust apportionment law, you are
again self-divested of the right to another, by the
neglect of your past legislature *to provide a remedy
for the evil.* To provide such a remedy, I believe
to be one of their most imperious duties to you.
That an effectual remedy is perfectly in their
power, the example of nearly every other state in
the Union testifies; and I can only express, as I
do, my earnest and anxious hope that not one
more session of your legislature shall be suffered
to pass without some provision of law which
shall secure to you at least the remnant of your
right to representation in the councils of the nation which the injustice of the present apportionment law has left you.

Let me not be understood as recommending the
principle, though sustained by the example of several states of the Union, that a simple plurality of
votes should be sufficient for an election. There
is among the temporary laws of the commonwealth a statute enacted in the year 1803, which
while it lasted did insure to you a full representation in congress; but it was suffered to expire,
rather by inadvertence than from any dissatisfac-
tion that was ever occasioned by it. To the prin-

ciple of requiring an absolute majority of votes I
would adhere so long as a reasonable hope of effecting it could be entertained; but after two un-
successful attempts I believe it would be a safer
expedient to terminate the contest even by draw-
ing lots for the choice, than by the protracted collisions and festering irritations of an interminable
struggle to turn the elective franchise into an
instrument of its own destruction.

Entertaining these opinions and holding these
principles, I consider the delegation to me of the
authority to represent in the national legislature,
the inhabitants of your twelfth congressional district, as a trust, to be fulfilled with diligence as
well as fidelity. Not one day—not one hour—of
voluntary absence from the discharge of the duties
incumbent on that trust have I permitted to myself during the twenty-second congress, nor shall
I permit to myself during the twenty-third. In
accepting the nomination of the convention at
Boston, it was therefore with the implied condition that it should in no wise interfere with the
fulfillment of my duties to my constituents of the
twelfth congressional district; and from the moment it was ascertained that an absolute majority
of the people of the commonwealth had not confirmed the nomination of the Antimasonic convention, my determination was taken. And this

determination was the more cheerfully made because the three other citizens between whom your suffrages are divided, and who will go as candidates nominated by you to the legislature, are all persons of ability and integrity, with whom I have the pleasure of being acquainted both in public and private life, and in whom I have great confidence. To yield to either of them any pretensions that I might have to your favor or that of your legislature, costs me not the slightest sacrifice; and after what I have said of Mr. Davis, it can not be improper for me to add that the preference which I should without hesitation assign to him, had I a vote in the election, would be as much in the indulgence of my own inclination as in deference to yours—it being evident to me from the comparative numbers of the returns that in the failure of an absolute majority of your suffrages for any one his share of them approaches the nearest to it, and must therefore be considered by me as most deserving of it.

In concluding this exposition of my own motives for assenting to the nomination of the Antimasonic convention, and now for withdrawing from the contest, let me give the parting advice of a friend to the remnant of the party styling themselves National Republicans, with whom I have generally concurred in opinion upon most of the great interests of the nation and of the commonwealth—though I have never professed to be one of them or of any other *party.* Let me exhort them to revise the political class-book, the elements of which confound the distinction between the meaning of the words *must* and *will.* Let them learn that it is not sufficient for a party to resolve that they *must* have a majority of votes, without using just and proper means to obtain it. Let them especially learn that to put down Antimasonry it is not enough for them dogmatically to tell you that *they* "look upon the Masonic fraternity as furnishing no cause for political strife."

The opinions of their addressing committee are no doubt of great weight upon subjects which they understand; but in the utter ignorance of the nature, character, and condition of the Masonic institution which their address displays, it is not from them that you will receive a dictation how you shall look upon it. They speak of Freemasonry as "an inefficient and almost superannuated institution." An institution which, at the moment when thus characterized by them, was convulsing all the free states of this Union; an institution in the support of which, under the transparent mask of neutrality, they were addressing you with pages of invective and slander upon its adversaries; an institution, under the shadow of whose wings they, and the convention whose voice they assumed to speak, were as effectively assembled as if every individual of them had drank the cup of the fifth libation! They tell you in the face of day, that Freemasonry is an inefficient and almost superannuated institution!

And since when is it inefficient and almost superannuated? Had the committee which penned that address heard the eloquent orator of the craft at New London, in July, 1825? He spoke of the then *present time*, and said, "It is powerful. It comprises men of rank, wealth, office, and talent, in power and out of power, and that in almost every place where power is of any importance. And it comprises among other classes of the community, to the lowest, in large numbers, active men united together, and capable of being directed by the efforts of others so as to have the force of concert throughout the civilized world. They are distributed too with the means of knowing one another, and the means of *co-operating*, in the desk, in the legislative hall, *on the bench*, in every gathering of business, in every part of pleasure, in every domestic circle, in peace and in war, among enemies and friends, in one place as well as in another."

Is this the inefficient and almost superannuated

institution of the committee? And upon this faithful Masonic representation of Masonic power, did you mark this concerted secret faculty of mutual recognition for the purposes of co-operation, in the legislative hall? Did you mark its ascent upon the very bench of justice? Is this the inefficient and almost superannuated institution? What *must* be the result of a mutual secret recognition for the purposes of co-operation between a judge on the bench, and a suitor or a culprit at the bar? Inquire of the records of the judicial tribunals of New York, and they will furnish the answer.

Has the institution, in the short space of time since the exhibition of this glowing picture of its power, been suddenly struck with inefficiency and superannuation? If the committee had consulted Masonic authority they would have found that the interval of fifteen months between the delivery of this discourse and the murder of William Morgan was one of unparalleled prosperity to the order, and unexampled multiplication of its members. Since the execution of the law of Masonry upon Morgan, by the co-operation, among others, *of the bench*, the institution has been, and continues to be, a church militant; and if in the prosecution of that warfare it has lost some of its efficiency, to whom and to what is this diminution of its power attributable? To Antimasonry—to *political Antimasonry* alone. All the measures taken to bring the murderers of Morgan and incendiaries of Miller's house to justice, were taken by political Antimasons. Almost all of them were defeated by the power of mutual recognition and co-operation upon *the bench*, and in the jury-box, and on the witnesses' stand. The disclosure of the Masonic oaths, obligations, and penalties was made by political Antimasons, seceders from the order. Political Antimasonry, and that alone, has prostrated the power of Masonry throughout the whole of that region of the State of New York where the most atrocious of her crimes had been committed. There, in the very center of her unhallowed. dominion, her scepter is broken, her voice is silenced, her hand is paralyzed; she is scotched, not killed. And so entirely does the existence, and of course all the evil, of political Antimasonry depend upon the active and mischievous existence of Masonry herself, that wherever she disappears, even but by hiding her face, political Antimasonry disappears with her. The people cease to consider either Masonry or Antimasonry as a test of qualification for office. Masons and Masonic adherents share the favor of the people in common with others, and then all the trumpets of Masonry where she still reigns sound the note of triumph that Anti-masonry is "dying away."

Political Antimasonry is founded upon a pure, precise, unequivocal principle *of morals.* That this is the Antimasonic cause the committee who addressed you against it dare not deny. Moral principle is the vital breath of Antimasonry. That a party thus originated and thus constituted should be traduced, slandered, and vilified by men having any pretension to morality of any kind themselves is not surprising, only because it corresponds with the general current of history and the ordinary operation of human passions.

Political Antimasonry sprung from the bosom of the people themselves; and it was the cry of horror from the unlearned, unsophisticated voice of the people at the murder of Morgan, at the prostration of law and justice in the impunity of his murderers, and at the disclosure of the Masonic obligations. That cry arose not from the mansions of the wealthy, nor from the cabinets of the learned or of the great, not even from the sentinels on the watch-towers of Zion; it came from the broad basis of the population—from the less educated and most numerous class of the community. So it is with all great moral reforms. When the gospel of peace itself was proclaimed, who was its founder? To worldly eyes, the son of a carpenter. Who were its apostles? Fishermen and toll-gatherers, publicans and sinners. Then the priest and the Levite, the Pharisee and the Sadducee, the Epicurean and the Stoic, the Roman governor and Jewish king, stood aloof, or *co-operated* in the crucifixion of the Savior. Not many wise men, not many mighty, not many noble, felt the efficacy of the call; and they who did immediately became the subject of every persecution and every indignity.

Let me draw no irreverent parallel, but the history of Christianity, in its secondary causes, is the history of all reformations of morals. It was by means of the *political* Antimasonic excitement that the spirit of reformation penetrated from the mass of the people into the bosom of the lodge, chapter, and encampment themselves.

The Le Roy conventions were composed of seceding Masons. The Dagan of the temple fell in the presence and by the hands of his own worshipers. If, then, Masonry has lost some portion of her efficiency since the boasting celebration of her power by her orator at New London, it is to political Antimasonry alone that this purification of the public morals must be ascribed. At this moment, between the convulsive struggles of Masonry to maintain in this commonwealth her empire; paramount to the laws, and the persevering

efforts of Antimasonry to redeem their supremacy, all the great parties in the state appear to be dissolving into their elements. Your
political divisions are becoming petty altercations
for men; all community of feeling and interest
in public concerns is shivering into rags. You
have been unable to concentrate your votes with
united energy sufficient to elect the ordinary
officers of your government. You have of your
own choice no governor, no lieutenant-governor,
scarcely a quorum of your Senate, and multitudes of the representatives of your towns have
failed to be elected by yourselves.

A long continuance of this state of things will
yield you and your interests to the mercy of those
associated with you in the national compact,—yet
feeling no sympathy with you, but much rather a
disposition to trample you under their feet. Of all
this *Freemasonry* is the cause. Let but the members of that fraternity within your borders convert their lodges into lyceums, and cease the administration of their oaths, and you may again be
a happy and united people. May it so please the
Supreme Disposer of events, prays, with every
sentiment of respect and gratitude to you.

Your friend and fellow-citizen.

JOHN QUINCY ADAMS.

APPENDIX.

The following are exact copies of the oaths, obligations, and penalties of the first three degrees in Masonry,—the Entered Apprentice, Fellowcraft, and the Master Mason,—extracted from the old manuscript mentioned in Colonel William L. Stone's Letters on Masonry and Antimasonry, Letter 7, page 67; and in the Appendix, p. 3, where it is said that while Morgan was at Rochester, these papers were there, and already written to his hands. For the more recent forms of oaths, see Bernard's work.

ENTERED APPRENTICE'S OBLIGATION.

I, A. B., do, of my own free will and accord, in the presence of God, and of this right worshipful Lodge, erected to God, and dedicated to holy St. John, hereby and hereon most solemnly and sincerely promise and swear.

That I will always hail, forever conceal, and never reveal, any of the secret or secrets of Masons or Masonry, which at this time, or at any time hereafter, shall be communicated to me as such, except it be to a true and lawful brother, or within the body of a just and regular Lodge, him or them whom I shall thus find to be, after strict trial and due examination.

I furthermore promise and swear that I will not write them, print them, stamp them, stain them, cut them, carve them, mark them, work or engrave them, nor cause them so to be done, upon anything movable or immovable under the canopy of heaven, capable of bearing the least visible sign, mark, character, or letter, whereby the mysteries of Masonry may be illegally obtained.

All this I solemnly and sincerely swear, with a full and hearty resolution to perform the same, without any evasion, equivocation, or mental reservation, under no less penalty than to have my throat cut across from ear to ear, my tongue plucked out by the roots, and buried in the rough sands of the sea, a cable's length from shore, where the tide ebbs and flows twice in twenty-four hours. So help me God, and keep me steadfast in this my obligation of an Entered Apprentice. K. once—(kiss the Bible once).

FELLOWCRAFT'S OBLIGATION.

I, A. B., do, of my own free will and accord, in the presence of God, and this right worshipful Lodge, erected to God, and dedicated to holy St. John, hereby and hereon most solemnly and sincerely promise and swear that I will always hail, forever conceal, and never reveal, any of the secret part or parts, mystery or mysteries, of a Fellowcraft to an Entered Apprentice: nor the part of an Entered Apprentice, or either of them, to any other person in the world, except it be to those to whom the same shall justly and legally belong.

327

I furthermore promise and swear that I will relieve all poor and indigent brethren, as far as their necessities require, and my ability will permit.

I furthermore promise and swear that I will obey all true signs, tokens, and summonses, sent me by the hand of a Fellowcraft, or from the door of a just and regular Fellowcraft s Lodge, if within the length of my cable-tow.

All this I solemnly and sincerely swear, with a full and hearty resolution to perform the same, without any evasion, equivocation, or mental reservation, under no less penalty than to have my heart taken from under my naked left breast, and carried to the valley of Jehosaphat, there to be thrown into the fields to become a prey to the wolves of the desert, and the vultures of the air. So help me God, &c. Kiss (the Bible) twice.

MASTER MASON'S OBLIGATION.

I, A. B., do, of my own free will and accord, in the presence of God, and of this right worshipful Lodge, erected to God, and dedicated to holy St. John, hereby and hereon most solemnly and sincerely promise and swear, that I will always hail, forever conceal, and never reveal, the secret part or parts, mystery or mysteries, of a Master Mason to a Fellowcraft, or those of a Fellowcraft to an Entered Apprentice, or them or either of them to any other person in the world, except it be to those to whom the same shall justly and legally belong.

I furthermore promise and swear that I will not be present at the making of a Mason of a woman, of a madman, or of a fool; that I will not defraud a brother knowingly or willingly; that I will not give the Master's words above breath, nor then except within the five points of fellowship;—that I will not violate the chastity of a Mason's wife or daughter, knowing them to be such.

I furthermore promise and swear, that I will attend a brother barefoot, if necessity requires, to warn him of approaching danger; that on my knees I will remember him in my prayers; that I will take him by the right hand and support him with the left in all his just and lawful undertakings; that I will keep his secrets as safely deposited in my breast as they are in his own, treason and murder only excepted, and those at my option; that I will obey all true signs, tokens, and summonses, sent me by the hand of a Master Mason, or from the door of a just and regular Master Mason's Lodge, if within the length of my cable-tow.

All this I most solemnly and sincerely promise and swear with a full and hearty resolution to perform the same, without any evasion, equivocation, or mental reservation, under no less penalty than to have my body cut across, my bowels taken out and burnt to ashes, and those ashes scattered to the four winds of heaven; to have my body dissected into four equal parts, and those parts hung on the cardinal points of the compass, there to hang and remain as a terror to all those who shall presume to violate the sacred obligation of a Master Mason. Kiss (the Bible) thrice.

These three penalties, the Master of the Lodge, immediately after administering this oath to the recipient Master Mason, declares to him, were *executed* upon the three Tyrian fellowcrafts, at the building of Solomon's temple, *and have ever since remained the standing penalties in the first three degrees of Masonry.*

The following form of the Royal Arch Oath, and that of the Knights Templar, are taken from the Boston edition of Avery Allyn's Ritual of Freemasonry, printed in 1831, pp. 143, 236.

ROYAL ARCH OATH.

I, A. B., of my own free will and accord, in presence of Almighty God, and this Chapter of Royal Arch Masons, erected to God and dedicated to Zerubbabel, do hereby and hereon, most solemnly and sincerely promise and swear, in addition to my former obligations, that I will not reveal the secrets of this degree to any of an inferior degree, nor to any being in the known world, except it be to a true and lawful companion Royal Arch Mason, or within the body of a just and legally constituted Chapter of such; and nev r unto him, or them, whom I shall hear so to be, but unto him and them only whom I shall find so to be, after strict trial and due examination, or lawful information given.

I furthermore promise and swear, that I will not wrong this Chapter of Royal Arch Masons, or a companion of this degree, out of the value of anything, myself, or suffer it to be done by others, if in my power to prevent it.

I furthermore promise and swear that I will not reveal the key to the ineffable characters of this degree, nor retain it in my possession, but will destroy it whenever it comes to my sight.

I furthermore promise and swear, that I will not speak the grand omnific Royal Arch word, which I shall hereafter receive, in any manner, except in that in which I shall receive it, which will be in the presence of three companion Royal Arch Masons, myself making one of the number; and then by *three times three*, under a living arch, and at low breath.

I furthermore promise and swear that I will not be at the exaltation of candidates in a clandestine Chapter, nor converse upon the secrets of this degree with a clandestine made Mason, or with one who has been expelled or suspended, while under that sentence.

I furthermore promise and swear, that I will not assist, or be present at the exaltation of a candidate to this degree, who has not received the degrees of Entered Apprentice, Fellowcraft, Master Mason, Mark Master, Past Master, and Most Excellent Master.

I furthermore promise and swear, that I will not be at the exaltation of *more* or *less* than *three* candidates, at one and the same time.

I furthermore promise and swear, that I will not be at the forming or opening of a Chapter of Royal Arch Masons, unless there be present nine regular Royal Arch Masons, myself making one of that number.

I furthermore promise and swear, that I will not speak evil of a companion Royal Arch Mason, behind his back, nor before his face, but will apprise him of all approaching danger, if in my power.

I furthermore promise and swear, that I will support the constitution of the Grand Royal Arch Chapter of the United States of America; together with that of the General Grand Chapter of this State, under which this Chapter is holden; that I will stand to, and abide by all the by-laws, rules, and regulations of this Chapter, or of any other Chapter of which I may hereafter become a member.

I furthermore promise and swear, that I will answer and obey all due signs and summons, handed, sent, or thrown to me from a Chapter of Royal Arch Masons, or from a companion Royal Arch Mason, if within the length of my cable-tow.

I furthermore promise and swear, that I will not strike a companion Royal Arch Mason, so as to draw his blood in anger.

I furthermore promise and swear, that *I will employ* a companion Royal Arch Mason, in *preference to any other person* of equal qualifications.

I furthermore promise and swear, that I will assist a companion Royal Arch Mason, when I see him engaged in *any* difficulty, and will *espouse his cause* so far as to *extricate* him from the same *whether he be RIGHT or WRONG.*

I furthermore promise and swear, that I will keep *all* the *secrets* of a companion Royal Arch Mason (when communicated to me as *such*, or I knowing them to be *such*,) *without exceptions.*

I furthermore promise and swear, that I will be aiding and assisting all *poor* and *indigent* companion Royal Arch Masons, their widows and orphans, *wheresoever dispersed around the globe;* they making application to me as such, and I finding them *worthy,* and can do it without *any material* injury to myself or family. To all which I do most solemnly and sincerely promise and swear, with a firm and steadfast resolution to keep and perform the same without any equivocation, mental reservation, or self-evasion of mind in me whatever; binding myself under no less penalty, than to have my *skull smote off,* and my *brains exposed to the scorching rays of the meridian sun,* should I knowingly or willfully violate, or transgress *any* part of this my solemn oath or obligation of a Royal Arch Mason. So help me God, and keep me steadfast in the due performance of the same. (Kissing the book seven times.)

KNIGHT TEMPLAR'S OATH.

I, A. B., of my own free will and accord, in the presence of Almighty God, and this Encampment of Knights Templars, do hereby and hereon most solemnly promise and swear that I will always hail, forever conceal, and never reveal, any of the secret arts, parts or points appertaining to the mysteries of this Order of Knights Templars, unless it be to a true and lawful companion Sir Knight, or within the body of a just and lawful Encampment of such; and not unto him, or them, until by due trial, strict examination, or lawful information, I find him or them lawfully entitled to receive the same.

Furthermore do I promise and swear, that I will answer and obey all due signs and regular summons which shall be given or sent to me from a regular encampment of Knights Templars, if within the distance of forty miles, natural infirmities and unavoidable accidents only excusing me.

Furthermore do I promise and swear, that I will help, aid, and assist with my counsel, my purse, and my sword, all poor and indigent Knights Templars, their widows and orphans, they making application to me as such, and I finding them worthy, so far as I can do it without material injury to myself, and so far as truth, honor, and justice may warrant.

Furthermore do I promise and swear, that I will not assist, or be present, at the forming and opening of an Encampment of Knights Templars, unless there be present seven Knights of the Order, or the representatives of three different Encampments, acting under the sanction of a legal warrant.

Furthermore do I promise and swear, that I will go to the distance of forty miles, even barefoot and on frosty ground, to save the life, and relieve the necessities of a worthy Knight, should I know that his necessities require it, and my abilities permit.

Furthermore do I promise and swear, that *I will wield my sword in the defense of innocent maidens, destitute widows, helpless orphans, and the Christian religion.*

Furthermore do I promise and swear, that I will support and maintain the by-laws of the Encampment of which I may hereafter become a member, the edicts and regulations of the Grand Encampment of the United States of America, so far as the same shall come to my knowledge; to all this I most solemnly and sincerely promise and swear, with a firm and steady resolution to perform and keep the same, without any hesitation, equivocation, mental reservation, or self-evasion of mind in me whatever; binding myself under no less penalty than to have my head struck off and placed on the highest spire in Christendom, should I knowingly or willingly violate any part of this my solemn obligation of a Knight Templar. So help me God, and keep me steadfast to perform and keep the same. (He kisses the book.)

FIFTH LIBATION

This part of the ceremony attending the creation of the Knight Templar, is deemed interesting in connection with the obligation.

Address of the Master.

Pilgrim, the fifth libation is taken in a very solemn way. It is emblematical of the bitter cup of death, of which we must all, sooner or later, taste; and even the Savior of the world was not exempted, notwithstanding his repeated prayers and solicitations. It is taken of pure wine, and from this cup. Exhibiting a human skull, he pours wine into it, and says: To show you that we here practice no imposition, I give you this pledge. (Drinks from the skull.) He then pours more wine into the skull, and presents it to the candidate, telling him that the *fifth libation* is called the sealed obligation, as it is to seal all his former engagements in Masonry.

If the candidate consents to proceed, he takes the skull in his hand, and repeats after the Most Eminent, as follows:

This pure wine I take from this cup, in testimony of my belief of the mortality of the body, and the immortality of the soul; and as the sins of the whole world were laid upon the head of our Savior, so may the sins of the person whose skull this once was, be heaped upon my head, in addition to my own; and may they appear in judgment against me, both here and hereafter, should I violate or transgress any obligation in Masonry, or the Orders of Knighthood which I have heretofore taken, take at this time, or may hereafter be instructed in. So help me God. (Drinks of the wine.)

The following extracts are referred to in Mr. Adams's fourth letter to Mr. Livingston, page 202.

Extracts from the Report made to the General Assembly of the State of Louisiana on the Plan of a Penal Code for the said State. By Edward Livingston.

"Legislators, in all ages and in every country, have at times endangered the lives, the liberties, and fortunes of the people by inconsistent provisions, CRUEL OR DISPROPORTIONATE PUNISHMENTS, and a legislation weak and wavering."

"Executions (in England) for some crimes were attended with BUTCHERY THAT WOULD DISGUST A SAVAGE."

"Acknowledged truths in politics and jurisprudence can never be too often repeated."

"Publicity is an object of such importance in free governments, that it not only ought to be permitted, but must be secured by a species of compulsion."

"If he (the culprit) be guilty, the state has an interest in his conviction; and whether guilty or innocent, it has a higher interest that the fact should be fairly canvassed before JUDGES INACCESSIBLE TO INFLUENCE AND UNBIASED BY ANY FALSE VIEWS OF OFFICIAL DUTY.

"It is not true, therefore, to say that the laws do enough, when they give the choice (even suppose it could be made with deliberation) between a fair and impartial trial and one that is liable to the strongest objections. They must do more; they must restrict that choice, so as not to suffer an ill-advised individual to dear do them into instruments of ruin, though it should be voluntarily inflicted, or of death, though that death should be suicide."

"The English mangle the remains of the dead (by suicide). The inanimate body feels neither the ignomy nor pains. The mind of the innocent survivor alone is lacerated by THIS USELESS AND SAVAGE BUTCHERY, and the disgrace of the execution is felt exclusively by him, although it ought to fall *on the laws which inflict it.*"

"The law punishes, not to avenge, but to prevent crimes. No punishments, greater than are necessary to effect this work of prevention, let us remember, ought to be inflicted."

"Although the dislocation of joints is no longer considered as the best mode of ascertaining innocence or discovering guilt; although offenses against the Deity are no longer expiated by the burning fagot; or those against the majesty of kings, avenged by the hot pincers and the rack and the wheel; still many other modes of punishment have their advocates, which, if not equally cruel, are quite as inconsistent with the true maxims of penal law."

"As to the authority of great names, it loses much of its force; since the mass of the people have begun to think for themselves."

"Where laws are so directly at war with the feelings of the people whom they govern, as this, and many other instances prove them to be, these laws can never be wise or operative, AND THEY OUGHT TO BE ABOLISHED."

Extracts from detached parts of the projected Code.

"No act of legislation can be, or ought to be, immutable.

"Vengeance is unknown to the laws. The only object of punishment is to prevent the commission of offenses."

"Penal laws should be written in plain language, clearly and unequivocally expressed, that they may neither be misunderstood nor perverted."

"The law never should command more than it can enforce. Therefore, whenever, from public opinion or any other cause, a penal law can not be carried into execution, it should be repealed."

"The legislature alone has a right to declare what shall constitute an offense."

www.ingramcontent.com/pod-product-compliance
Lightning Source LLC
Chambersburg PA
CBHW021119270326
41929CB00009B/947